MAKING MEN WHOLE

By J. B. Phillips

LETTERS TO YOUNG CHURCHES
A translation of the New Testament Epistles
THE GOSPELS *translated into Modern English*
YOUR GOD IS TOO SMALL
MAKING MEN WHOLE

J. B. PHILLIPS

Making Men Whole

New York
THE MACMILLAN COMPANY

Seventh Printing, 1962

PRINTED IN THE UNITED STATES OF AMERICA

CONTENTS

FOREWORD

THE FOLLOWING FIVE CHAPTERS REPRESENT THE SUBSTANCE OF THE Bible Readings which I was asked to give during the first week of the Church Missionary Society Summer School at Bangor in 1952. The title, *Making Men Whole,* represents the dominant thought of our prayer and study together. As an introduction to the appearance of these Bible Readings in book form, I would underline the following points which seem to me basic to our theme:

1. Many Christians suffer to-day, more perhaps than in any preceding age, from a sense that the world is out of control. The impact of world tensions and problems is often so great that Christians, because they see and feel and care more than non-Christians, frequently become over-anxious and exaggerate their own responsibilities. We all need to be reminded that God is by no means baffled or bewildered by mankind's muddles and follies. We all need to remember that our strength lies in quietness and confidence, not in frantic challenges and hysterical efforts. The world remains primarily God's responsibility, and the best we can do is to find out our own part in His vast purpose and make sure that we are fulfilling that to the limit of our ability.

2. Most Christians are affected far more than they know by the standards and methods of the surrounding world. In these days when power and size and speed are almost universally admired, it seems to me particularly important to study afresh the "weakness," the "smallness of entry" and the "slowness" of God as He began His vast work of reconstructing His disordered world.

We are all tempted to take short cuts, to work for quick results and to evade painful sacrifice. It is therefore essential that we should look again at love incarnate in a human being, to see God Himself at work within the limitations of human personality, and to base our methods on what we see Him do.

3. The writers of the New Testament Epistles never regarded the Christian religion as an "ethic," still less a performance. To them it was an invasion of their own lives by the living Spirit of God; their response in repentance and faith provided the means by which the divine could penetrate the merely human. They lived lives of super-human quality because they believed quite simply that Christ Himself was alive within them.

For some reason or other we seem to regard this belief as somewhat presumptuous, and much of our present-day Christianity is a rather gauche performance designed to please an external God. The real presumption, indeed the impertinence, of our modern attitude is that we do not really accept God's full generosity; we do not really believe that Christ is alive and operative in every true disciple.

4. The pressure of world events, as well as of the gentle leading of the Spirit of God Himself, is making it plain to the dimmest human intelligence that men must learn to live together as one family or perish from the earth altogether. Thus I believe that we can say, without unduly dramatizing ourselves, that we live in a time of great acceleration of God's "one increasing purpose." In Christ alone is there integration for the individual, for the Churches, and for the whole scattered human family. The purpose itself, in its scope and depth, is becoming clearer, and the most important issue confronting any one of us is the question: "Am *I* co-operating with the purpose, or not?"

5. If we are to have a "whole" view of life and its purpose, it is very necessary for us to recover the sense that this human life of ours is lived *sub specie aeternitatis.* In our modern preoccupation with Christian social justice and the relevance of the Christian faith to all human problems, we tend to forget the heaven to

which we are bound. Unless we have this essential background, we are left with too many unsolved problems and too many flagrant injustices for us to believe confidently in the love of God. Quite apart from the question of rewards, punishments and compensations, we do not allow God sufficient "elbow-room" in this restricted sphere for the final working out of His awful patient purpose. We must recover the wonder and glory of the calling wherewith we are called.

Nothing that I have written is new; all of it is based on the Scripture passages which are at the head of each chapter. But we need constantly to be reminded of those eternal truths by which alone we can face this life with courage, hope and good humour.

J. B. Phillips

St. John's Vicarage
Redhill, Surrey

I

God and a World Disintegrated

Passages which should be studied in connexion with the following chapter are:

ST. JOHN x. verses 1 to 16
EPHESIANS ii. verses 4 to 18

I

God and a World Disintegrated

We face to-day a world torn and divided. So widespread is the distress of nations, so complex the problems which face every thinking Christian, that I think we may be forgiven if our hearts sometimes fail us. There is no need to elaborate here the problems and distresses which confront us on every hand. Probably we are only too well aware of them. But for our comfort we may fairly remind ourselves that the world-wide tensions and sufferings only seem to us to be more overwhelming than they did to our forefathers because we are much better informed about them through modern means of news-transmission than they could ever be. To-day, with vastly improved communications of all kinds, we are aware of what is happening in distant places, whereas our forefathers could live much more parochially and usually with little sense of world problems.

This difference is not, of course, entirely a matter of news-communication, for during the last century the nations have become infinitely more inter-dependent than ever before in the history of the world. To be isolationist or parochial has become not only un-Christian but impossible. What happens in China, or Africa or the United States can no longer be of merely academic interest to us; it can affect profoundly our actual lives. A hundred years ago or less, it would have been fantastic to suggest that a struggle in far-off Korea, for example, could have the faintest bearing on the private life of an ordinary Englishman, even if he knew about it. To-day we are so inter-related that the problems of distant countries affect not merely our minds and hearts but our very mode of living, whether we like it or not. In days gone by there could be famines, plagues, bitter wars, earthquakes and disasters, happening perhaps on a vast scale in a far-away continent, and we should have known nothing of them. But to-day we hear of these things, we read of them, we see pictures of them on the news-reels, and even the least sensitive can hardly say, "This is no concern of mine."

To put it another way, the vast achievements of science through improved travelling, and communications have borne in upon the sensitive soul, and more slowly upon the insensitive, the fact that we are, however divided, "all in it together." There has never been a time in the history of the world when men have thought and calculated in global terms as to-day they must. And there is, of course, no arresting of this progress, no preventing of the awakening from sleep of continent and race. We as Christians are probably more sensitive than anyone else to the fact that for the first time in the history of the human race men have got to learn to live together as a family. And because we know how deep-rooted are human sins and frailties, we are more aware than others of how difficult this problem must inevitably be.

We need not, however, be overwhelmed by the prospect before us, for two reasons. First, because this is God's world, and although we may be bewildered by the speed at which the world is awakening before our eyes, we can be quite sure that there is no bewilderment in the mind of God. This is His world; and since He knows the end from the beginning we can at all times be confident that at any given moment in the world's history there is, for those who will listen to His voice, a right way of meeting the complexities of the contemporary situation, even though that right way cannot in the nature of things achieve in a single generation the perfect will of God.

Then again, we need constantly to remind ourselves that no single one of us and no single group of us is required to carry more responsibility than we can bear. We may well feel battered, bruised and bewildered by the continual assault of news, of problems put before us, of challenges thrown down to us. But each man has his proper work to do, and no single one of us is required to do more than the will of God for him. The famous words, "In His will is our peace," are perfectly true here as in other contexts. If we attempt to do more than His will, if we allow ourselves to be stampeded into responsibilities beyond our powers by the vastness of the problems around us, we lose our peace. We need, as St. Paul told the Thessalonians, "to study to be quiet and to do our business" (1 Thessalonians iv. 11). In doing our part of God's will we shall find peace, but in attempting more than our part we shall find only anxiety and frustration.

This truth needs to be thought out by all who share a common interest in the world-wide work of the Church. We can so easily become tense and over-anxious just because we are sensitive to the world's need, and thereby fail effectually to do that small part of the task which God has allotted to us. Because of the magnitude of the problems which press upon us, we may even seek to evade such frightening responsibilities. But if we will keep in mind the fact that the ultimate responsibility belongs to God and be willing to accept not the whole of the world's burden but that part which God has marked out for us to carry, we shall be able to accept His call to maintain our peace and do our work effectually.

It is necessary to point out that our responsibility is a relative one only, for as we think of the world-wide disintegration of the human family the prospect before us could easily fill us with alarm and despondency, if we were not sure first of the absolute sovereignty of God, who (I speak reverently) knows what He is doing in conducting this enormous experiment that we call life.

Secondly, though we often think in terms of world issues, the majority of us are not called to be world leaders or anything like it, but sensible and faithful servants of the One whose purpose it is to unite the scattered races under one Shepherd.

In St. John x. our Lord contrasts Himself as the *Good* Shepherd in whose care the sheep find food and security, with the thieves and robbers who came before Him. I have often wondered whom He had in mind, for the words as they stand, "All that came before me are thieves and robbers" (St. John x. 8), sound rather harsh. It is probable that in the contemporary situation Christ had in mind leaders of men, political, national and even religious, who really, in the long run, destroyed or stole for their own ends the souls of men. There are many "thieves and robbers" in the situation to-day who are similarly exploiting and destroying personality. We think of the soul-destroying aims and methods of Communism, of false religions which ask so much of men and in the end give them nothing. We think of the blight of materialism which by flattering a man's importance in this life deprives him of his destiny as a son of God. We think of the reckless pursuit of pleasure which meets man's love of beauty and happiness with the tawdry and the meretricious.

Within a man's own personality there is no lack of "thieves and robbers." There is his driving ambition which without the influence of Christ becomes, sooner or later, a destructive tyrant; there is his pride which insulates him from his neighbour and sows enmity between his group and another. Above all, there is his fear, rooted of course in pride and self-love, which drives out the milk of human kindness and which in its extreme forms makes him behave far worse than the animal creation. We have to face the fact that in the individual man as well as in society there have always been these disintegrating factors, the "thieves and robbers" who, though often unseen, are quietly at work. Yet wherever He is given the chance, there is the integrating factor, the Good Shepherd Himself, seeking to make men whole, seeking to integrate both human personality and the whole human family.

The problem of making men whole, of integrating them as persons and unifying them in a community, is much more difficult than some idealists might suppose. The "thieves and robbers," the disintegrating forces, have had a very long innings. They are deeply entrenched, their cumulative infection is overwhelming, and they are by no means always recognized for what they are. It is quite literally a superhuman task to plunge into the welter of centuries of disintegration and begin to make men whole.

At the risk of repetition, it must be emphasized that what we are beginning to envisage nowadays is a much larger-scale and more widespread integration than our forefathers as a general rule imagined. The salvation of an individual soul is indeed important, but we are beginning to see that the work of the Good Shepherd goes deeper and wider than we ever supposed. It is true that His plan considers the importance of the single "sheep"; under the Good Shepherd the one sheep can be saved and "go in and go out and find pasture" (St. John x. 9). But the plan is far greater than that. There are the "other sheep" (St. John x. 16) at present astray, who must also be brought into the fold. It is not only the so-called contemporary pressures which make us feel that we are "all in this together"; to those who are sensitive to the breath of the Spirit it is surely God Himself who is widening our horizons, mentally and spiritually, and making us feel and see the breath-taking compass of His integrating purpose.

Nothing less than a world-wide principle of wholeness, a world-loving and world-loved King and Shepherd, will suffice for our modern need. In the past, so long as men were broken up into more or less self-contained units, it was not altogether impossible to secure an integration which was local and to some extent superficial. The rules and customs of a tribe, for example, the unquestioned but purely parochial authority of their king, priest or leader produced such a limited "wholeness." In our own country, there sometimes existed in a village, for example, such a circumscribed integration. And no doubt in many countries a similar local harmony was often achieved. But the need to-day, as is obvious to anyone with eyes to see, is for something at once more penetrating and more far-reaching than that limited conception. Indeed, on examination we find that the apparent wholeness of little communities was due at least in part to fear of other communities; and the very loyalty which preserved the local cohesion would effectually prevent co-operation with similar communities. In our Lord's day, for example, there was a certain cohesive loyalty about the Jews which produced in both personality and community some magnificent results. Yet it was exclusive, "for Jews have no dealings with Samaritans" (St. John iv. 9), and they regarded the Gentiles with, at the best, a tolerant contempt. We hardly realize the explosive quality of St. Paul's inspiration when, under the influence of the new integrating force, he declared that in Christ there can be "neither Jew nor Greek, there can be neither bond nor free, there can be no male and female" (Galatians iii. 28).

It may be a little presumptuous and it may be a little premature, but it seems to me that in this twentieth century, with the whole inhabited world awakening and opening up before our eyes, we have the chance for the first time to see the vastness of God's integrating plan. The apparent insignificance of its beginning is breath-taking. For if we strip away for a moment the romance and decoration of the Christmas story, we stand aghast at the awe-inspiring humility of God's beginning of His task of integration. The things which look romantic on a Christmas card or which sound pretty by association with delightful carols were in fact most devastatingly humble. For a pregnant woman to hunt desperately for a room when her time drew near would hardly be our choice for God's entry into the world on human terms! And yet so it was. That is how He came, right in at the human level: the Word of wholeness was born into a world of misery and strife, of suffering and sin.

It is the temptation not only of politicians and law-makers, but of religious people as well, to think that people can be made whole and that they can be induced to live together in harmony, by fiats of authority. Yet when God began His work of personal rescue, there was no trump from heaven, there were no supporting armies of angels. In the Man who was God in human form, God focused and scaled down to meet our human need, we find One "meek and lowly in heart," who allowed the thieves and robbers of humanity to close in upon Him and kill Him. He had, He has, a frightening patience; frightening, that is, to us who have so little faith and have such a lust for quick results. But the work of making men whole was begun.

Although the coming of the integrating principle into a dark, perplexed and infected world began, so to speak, on the ground level, can we not begin to see that this is, without qualification, the only way in which God, or for that matter any power whatsoever, could restore wholeness to mankind? Every effort to impose wholeness by regulation from above must fail, partly because it is for ever external to human nature itself; partly because it neither excites the love nor provides the power to overcome human spiritual poverty. St. Paul was right when he said the law "was weak" (Romans viii. 3). When it attempted to change human nature it was not weak in one sense, in that it represented the eternal principles of human conduct. But it was completely powerless in practice because of its utter incapacity to change man's nature from within.

In Ephesians ii. St. Paul speaks with confidence, having observed the result of God's method through Christ. Into human life and at the human level, He, so to speak, inserts His own life with its immeasurable potentialities for converting, redeeming, reconciling and bringing into harmony. From the world's point of view, this low-level approach was and still is a ridiculously weak and impracticable way of tackling the deep-rooted problems of human nature. Yet it has worked, not invariably and not without failure, but with a result so impressive that even a hostile world cannot disregard it. New powers, new qualities, a new spirit came to birth and began at once to work upon even the most unpromising material to produce whole men, and of humanity a Whole Man. The process has continued ever since, and though our faith is small and our experience limited we have all seen things happen which were never possible in a pagan world. With this astonishing apparent weakness God is at work with a kind of loving relentlessness to make "in himself . . . one new man, so making peace" (Ephesians ii. 15).

There then are the two contrasting energies at work, marring or making for wholeness in the lives of men: on the one hand the big noisy, apparently unconquerable passions of the world, which are the "thieves and robbers" of man's true nature; and on the other the quiet, gentle, but immensely powerful work of the Good Shepherd.

But there is something vital to add, in terms of man's response. The Church began with the supernaturally inspired insight of Peter who cried, "Thou art the Christ, the Son of the living God" (St. Matthew xvi. 16). Up to that moment, if we may look at things reverently from Christ's point of view, there had been swirling tides of emotion among the people whom He met. Popular enthusiasm ran high; He was the great Healer, He was the wonderful Teacher, He was a reincarnation of one of the prophets of old. But all this was an unreliable floating tide of opinion. Then came Peter's inspired remark, and at once our Lord (God walking the earth as a human being) seized upon the solidity of real faith. "You are Peter, the Rock-man!" He cried out, in delight, I think, "and upon this rock I will build my church" (St. Matthew xvi. 18). To Christ's matchless insight here was the beginning of this worldwide fellowship of men and women of all races. Here was the tiny beginning of the society which would transcend all barriers of colour, class and custom, yes, and even time and space as well. For Peter, in a moment of true faith, had seen who Christ really was.

To see and to recognize who Jesus Christ really was and is makes the whole vast work of rescue possible. Prophets, poets, idealists, all have their message to give, but until someone sees that God Himself has penetrated into human life at man's own level there can be no real beginning to the work of making men whole. Without this recognition there is no certainty, only a feeling. Without this recognition there is no ultimate certainty, only a hopeful idealism. Without this certainty there is no observable purpose in all the ills and accidents, the injustices and the bitter disappointment in this transitory part of existence that we call life. But once this recognition has come to birth, the certainty is there, the guarantee is there, the power is there; the authority, the plan and the purpose are all there, and the building can begin. No wonder Christ said of Peter's outburst of faith, "upon *this* rock I will build my church."

It is most noteworthy that this certainty runs right through the New Testament. It is as though men were using then a faculty which to-day is largely atrophied, the faculty of faith. They were not so much holding on desperately despite the evidence of a hostile world—their faith amounted to knowledge. They knew: they knew God; they knew the purpose and plan of God; they knew the power of God. And although from our modern point of view their outlook was restricted, in many ways they could see further than we, and by the inspiration of the Spirit of God they gained more than a glimpse of the majestic sweep of God's vast purpose. Before we can move in the matter, before we can be made whole ourselves or take an active, telling part in the work of making men whole, we have to recapture that certainty. It is true that we are surrounded on all sides by uncertainty, but so were they. It is true that we are confronted by all kinds of evil, by a world at sixes and sevens with itself, but so were they. We may be sure that God has not changed, nor has His purpose been altered by the centuries. I confess I can see no valid reason why we should not use that faculty to grasp "the substance of things hoped for, the evidence of things not seen" (Hebrews xi. 1. A.V.). This is not a modern problem, though modern pressures have almost persuaded us that it is. It would be a great thing if God could show each one of us that we still have that faculty of faith, puny and underdeveloped though it may be, and teach us how greatly He could work if we could cease from our anxieties and our preoccupations and reach out to contact the unseen but thoroughly dependable realities.

We need then first of all to recapture Christian certainty which is not a superior form of wishful thinking, but a regrasping of the purpose and plan of God by a faculty which, though long disused, is implanted in every child of God.

II

The action and the aim of love

The passage which should be studied in connexion with the following chapter is:

I JOHN iv. verses 7 to the end

II

The action and the aim of love

St. Paul once said that "faith cometh by hearing and hearing by the word of God," and that is a most important statement. For it implies that we have within us not merely the power for holding on to a set of ideas which we believe to be good, but also the faculty for grasping and comprehending the truth of God. To many somewhat depressed Christians to-day there comes at times the feeling that they are clinging to an interpretation of life which they believe to be the truth, but which the world around regards as merely one of many interpretations. This is an unnecessarily depressed attitude, for the Christian is by faith reaching out and touching the real world. He is in contact with the "substance of things hoped for" (Hebrews xi. 1. A.V.). For the word of God which stimulates and sustains faith is eternal truth breaking through into this temporary world, so that the certainty of the early Christians which we may regard with a certain wistfulness means, not that they were necessarily men of exceptional spiritual calibre, but simply that they recognized the word of God as being quite literally the message, plan and command of God Himself. It was a faith more rock-like than any human certainty which gave their lives their astonishing quality.

To-day we need to purge ourselves of any lingering thoughts that the Christian Gospel (and the spreading of that Gospel) is simply a good idea to be held tenaciously rather as men will hold on to a political theory. It is infinitely more than this; we hold in our hands "the word of life" (Philippians ii. 16). We share, incredible as it may seem, part of the plan of God Himself; to some extent we are even in His confidence, for we know something of His methods and the vast scope of His purpose.

In the midst then of human conflicts, tensions and sufferings, there comes to those who believe the word of God far more than an inkling of what God is attempting. Once we accept Jesus Christ as the planned focusing of God in history, our faith becomes a certainty and we know, not indeed the whole of God, but what sort of Person God is, what kind of plan He is attempting to work out, and what sort of people we ought to be in co-operating with that purpose. We learn how *we* may be made whole; we learn along which lines the world may be made whole; and to us is given something far more than the ability to stand in this faith. We are, as St. Paul said, "more than conquerors through him that loved us" (Romans viii. 37), so that we win no bare victory against the world, the flesh and the devil merely by the skin of our teeth. God gives us the power and the love to overflow into the world about us.

Let us remind ourselves then of the character of God, the methods of God, and the resources of God. Our authority for these reminders is the New Testament, which is not only an unique collection of historical documents containing the record of the actual physical life of God when He became man, and of the actual demonstrable results which followed when men, by His Spirit, lived out His way of life. The New Testament is uniquely inspired because through these human, unselfconscious documents there comes again and again the authentic word of God—truths breaking through like shafts of light from the real eternal world into the darkness of this temporary one.

The beginning of our certainty, the conviction that lies behind the task of making men and nations whole, lies in three simple words written by St. John, namely, "God is love" (1 John iv. 8 and 16). I sometimes wish we could appreciate this, the primal fact of all existence, with fresh and unprejudiced minds, for there are several difficulties which stand in the way of our accepting this statement at its face value—which is surely what we should do.

First, in modern parlance the word "love" has become demoted and indeed debased to mean all sorts of things. A man can have a love for Beethoven's string quartets and a love for chocolates with hard centres; he can love driving an open car at high speed; but when he wants to express what he feels for the One who has touched the deepest roots of his being, and wants, as all lovers do, to declare himself, he can only use the same word! Whether it is due to paucity of language or mere carelessness, we find the same word used for a romantic but passing affection as for a lifetime's devotion and service. Yet the image of God is by no means altogether defaced in mankind, and a great many people, though they use the word carelessly or even sentimentally, have some idea of what love really means. Their deepest experiences are all strongly connected with love, and even the careless and the superficial quite frequently have a wistful admiration for genuine love.

The second difficulty is that men have been afraid to proclaim in its astonishing vulnerability the love of God. Its generosity is indeed awe-inspiring, but in putting our message before men we have no right so to qualify the love of God, so to surround it with caveats and provisos, that it ceases to be love at all in the commonly accepted meaning of the term. Jesus once declared that God is "kind toward the unthankful and evil" (St. Luke vi. 35), and even I remember preaching a sermon on this text to a horrified and even astounded congregation who simply refused to believe (so I gathered afterwards) in this astounding liberality of God. That God should be in a state of constant fury with the wicked seemed to them only right and proper, but that God should be kind towards those who were defying or disobeying His laws seemed to them a monstrous injustice. Yet I was but quoting the

Son of God Himself, and I would only comment here that the terrifying risks that God takes are part of His nature. We do not need to explain or modify His unremitting love towards mankind.

Then again we have the distressing phenomenon exhibited by some Christians of love in inverted commas! "Let love be without hypocrisy," wrote St. Paul (Romans xii. 9), and I sometimes wonder whether he had this imitation love in mind. I think I know how it comes about. Christians are commanded to love, and unless they allow their own hearts to be both humbled and purged by the vast love of God they are likely to exhibit a purely superficial attitude of love towards those who are not Christians, or even towards Christians who are not of their school of thought. They cannot really bear to be vulnerable, as love always must be; to be imposed upon, humiliated or ridiculed, as love often may be. Yet not only do they impoverish their own lives; they are at least partly responsible for the impression which many people have that Christian love is somehow not quite genuine, and that when Christians declare that God is love they mean that behind a smiling providence He hides a frowning face!

Somehow Christians must recapture on a grand scale this basic certainty that God *is* love. Unless they do, unless they feel it and know it and show it and live it, it is unlikely that the surrounding world, burdened by the apparent contradictions and all the ills and accidents of this mortal life, will ever grasp the fundamental fact of all creation.

If we were to study, without preconceived ideas, the life of Christ as recorded in the Gospels; if with fresh minds we could consider that life fairly and squarely, I am certain that we should be very surprised. So much is read back into the story, so much majesty and even solemnity is added by the matchless beauty of the Authorized Version, that I doubt whether many of us have had an unencumbered and unprejudiced view of incarnate love. Yet I believe we ought to try, even if it means a stern effort of will and the free exercise of our God-given imagination.

Let me mention three salient points among many which baffled and bothered the early disciples and which baffle and bother us—until we see that God really did enter unarmed at our own level and that He is really love, and not someone pretending to be love with a big stick within easy reach!

(1) His attitude towards "sinners." To the religious people of His day it was a scandalous thing that Jesus, unlike the prophets of old, made no denunciation of those who were called sinners; and we too may find it, if not scandalous, at least surprising. Jesus almost never called men sinners, except in the case of the entrenched self-righteous, whom we shall consider in a moment. Perhaps I make this point clearer if, speaking for myself, I say that a high-pressure evangelist, whose technique depended on arousing and fostering a sense of guilt, would find himself woefully short of ammunition if he were only allowed to use as his texts the recorded words of Christ. With the common run of ordinary sinners, Jesus appears to have used the method of simple love. The sense of guilt, it would appear, might well take care of itself; so far as we can judge He did not attempt to arouse it. Consequently, we find Matthew, loved and appreciated as a man perhaps for the first time for many years, giving up a profitable racket and following One who called him in love. We find Zaccheus, whose keen business instincts had shut him off from love and friendship, instantly melting into astonishing generosity when love touched his life. We find the hard woman of the streets, who had possibly never known anything but simulated love, breaking down completely before the One who loved her as a daughter of God. Even the woman taken in adultery was defended in her terrible exposure by the Son of God Himself, and assured that He did not condemn her.

This method of making people whole by outflowing love was and is extremely risky, but it was a risk that Jesus was prepared to take. And we may infer that God is prepared to take this the chief risk among all the other risks that He has taken in giving man free will.

Of course, even the perfect methods of perfect love did not invariably succeed. But I am drawing attention not to results —much as the modern world is hypnotized by "results"—but to the divine method. No doubt, to the early disciples as they began to realize Who it was that they were following, the method appeared foolish, dangerous and even wrong. James and John were by no means unique in wanting to call down fire from heaven (St. Luke ix. 54) upon the village that would not receive incarnate love; while, on the other hand, Peter was sharply rebuked for suggesting that some less dangerous and less uncompromising way might be found than the way of vulnerable love in an evil world (St. Matthew xvi. 23). The single clear purpose of Christ could never admit that either fire from heaven or the avoiding of suffering could ultimately heal man's evil plight. The methods of Christ, which are the methods of God, are certainly not our normal methods, and if we want to co-operate with His purpose we should do well to study His ways.

(2) The second remarkable fact that emerges from the Gospel records is the enmity of the religious. There is a chapter in Professor Thomas Jessop's book *Law and Love* with the provoking title "The Badness of Goodness"; it explains with the utmost clarity why it was not the publicans and sinners, but those whose life-long purpose was to lead good lives, who, by a strange paradox, became the deadly enemies of God in human form. It is, I think, a mistake to suppose that all the Pharisees, for example, were self-righteous humbugs whose unreality and hypocrisy Jesus mercilessly exposed. It would be truer to say that they were men ruled by principle, often with a great many conspicuous virtues; but they differed from Christ fundamentally in that the mainspring of their lives lay in observing the law and keeping their own souls unspotted from the world, while His lay in loving His Father with the whole of His being, and His fellow men with the same love that He knew was eternally at the heart of His Father. Their religion was a kind of contract, a *quid pro quo* performance, while His was the spontaneous outliving of unadulterated

love. It must often have looked to them as though He were ready to drive a coach and six through the law and the prophets. But in fact He went far above and beyond any "righteousness" that the law could produce. When directly challenged, He declared that the whole of the prophet's message and the law's morality depended upon the two most important commandments, namely, to love God with the whole of the personality, and to love one's neighbour as oneself (St. Matthew xxii. 38–40). St. Paul, seeing the same truth in a slightly different way—and not, I think, ever quite able, despite his protestations, to shake himself completely free from the Law in which he was nurtured—declared, "Love therefore is the fulfilment of the law" (Romans xiii. 10).

It would be a profound mistake to suppose that all the Pharisees disappeared soon after the death of Christ, or that they have no heirs and successors to-day. Indeed, it is true that there is much of the Pharisee in each one of us, and by that I do not mean that we are hypocrites, but simply that we would rather reduce religion to a code, both inward and outward, than take the tremendous risk of being invaded by and becoming part of vulnerable but relentless love. We do not have to look far to find Christians who have tamed and regulated something that can in fact neither be tamed nor regulated. We do not like risks; we do not like being hurt or disappointed; and there is in us all something of the spirit which would rather label and condemn and bewail than love and suffer and perhaps redeem. We smile as we read of Peter's attempt to regulate the illimitable. "If I have got to forgive," he said, "could we not regard seven times as the maximum?" (St. Matthew xviii. 21). But the same spirit is in us, and perhaps we have not yet seen how vast and humble and magnificent and generous is the love of God, nor have we realized that we are to be "perfect as He is perfect" (St. Matthew v. 48). Yet until we have some realization of this illimitable love of God, we shall never understand the conflict between "religion" and the Son of God, observed and recorded for our learning.

(3) The third surprising and rather disquieting side of God's

activity while He was on earth as incarnate love, was His refusal to use supernatural advantages or to interfere with man's free choice by the use of divine power. We know, for instance, that at one period the disciples confidently expected an earthly kingdom to be set up, and although their hopes of this became more and more deferred, yet His death came to them as a kind of "end-of-the-world" disaster, so that every loyalty was driven out by their fear and disappointment. And His appearances after the Resurrection were to men broken-hearted and utterly demoralized by the collapse of their hopes. Despite His constant reminders that His Kingdom was a spiritual kingdom, it appears that somehow they expected Him to take the power and reign. It is true that only one of the twelve experienced such a bitter reversal of his hopes that he was prepared to betray the One he loved for a paltry sum of cash, but of the others, in their hour of desolation, one denied him publicly three times, and the others "left him, and fled" (St. Matthew xxvi. 56 and 70).

I am far from judging the disciples harshly, and I would be slow to suggest that you and I would have behaved any differently in the circumstances, but I find the wholesale desertion at the end of Christ's life an almost certain indication that they could not understand this basic fact about God: He does not use force to accomplish His purpose. I hope I am not being unduly imaginative when I suggest that it must have crossed their minds many times in those last dark days that it would literally be the easiest thing in the world for God to intervene and prevent the murder of His perfect Son. What a justification of His claims, what a demonstration of the power of light over darkness, what a rousing victory for the God who had visited His people! But no celestial rescue party left the courts of heaven, no angel interfered in the final tragedy. And in the last blackness He cried, "My God, my God, why hast thou forsaken me?" (St. Matthew xxvii. 46).

It is, of course, easy for us to be wise after the event and to know that "thus it must be" (St. Matthew xxvi. 54). But I think it is still true that we are puzzled by the apparent inaction of God. From the crude cry which we heard so often during the war years, "If there is a God, why doesn't He stop Hitler?" to the unspoken questioning in many a Christian heart when a devoted servant of Christ dies from accident or disease at what seems to us a most inopportune moment, there is this universal longing for God to intervene, to show His hand, to vindicate His purpose. I do not pretend to understand the ways of God any more than the next man, but it is surely more fitting as well as more sensible for us to study what God does do and what He does not do as He works in and through the complex fabric of this disintegrated world, than to postulate what we think God ought to do and then feel demoralized and bitterly disappointed because He fails to fulfil what we expect of Him. I am certain that God who is our Father and understands us perfectly views, if I may dare to say so, with the utmost sympathy our desires to see evil dramatically punished, or at least prevented, and good triumphantly vindicated and conspicuously rewarded. But hard though it is, He has to teach us that He will no more interfere with other people's freedom than He does with our own.

I do not, however, want to leave you with a picture of a world at the mercy of the evil forces within it, and into which God never penetrates because He has promised not to interfere. The true picture is that of a world granted the immense and risky gift of free will, which is at all times surrounded by the love of God. While it is true that God forces His way into no man's personality, yet He is always ready, where the right conditions are fulfilled, to enter and redeem and transform. The chief of the right conditions is what the New Testament calls faith; the willingness to use the faculty which can touch God and which can, as it were, provide an opening through which the ever-present loving purpose can enter and operate. This love may seem to us remote and inactive, but that is because we forget the conditions under which it can operate, because we forget its incredible humility, as well as under-estimate its true power. Because we all tend to model our ideas of God upon what we see of men, we imagine that He who has the most power will of necessity most obviously demonstrate that power. But if we model our idea of the character of God upon what we see of Jesus Christ, we have a very different picture. We see the astounding humility of God who "stands at the door and knocks" (Revelation iii. 20), and will not enter until He is invited. We see a character not in the least concerned with demonstrations of the kind of power which impress men superficially, but fully ready to supply any number of demonstrations of inward transformation, of arousing love and hope and enthusiasm, and of providing adequate resources for carrying through the inward spiritual task.

One further comment: St. John declares that "every one that loveth is begotten of God, and knoweth God" (1 John iv. 7). And indeed, a whole sermon could be preached on that pregnant sentence. But I use it here as a kind of tail-piece to show that this love of God, of which we have been thinking and of which so much can be expected, is not so different in quality that we cannot recognize it as love when we meet it. It is love, our old familiar friend, higher and better, more splendid and more generous, but still love, the most precious thing that we know, the quality which even in our duller moments we know can outlast anything. It is not so much that we do not understand what love is, but that we are slow to grasp love's methods of working. We are tempted by love of power, by the show of results, by the short cut, by the pleasing exterior; but love is deceived by none of these things and takes awful patient ways, of which we know very little. Yet, though we are blind and ignorant and stupid, it is of unspeakable comfort and gives rise to unspeakable hope in our hearts to know, not only that God is wonderful and beautiful and good, but that He actually is that strange quality which lives in our inmost heart —love itself.

III

The work of reconciliation

Passages which should be studied in connexion with the following chapter are:

2 CORINTHIANS v. verses 14 to the end, and 2 CORINTHIANS vi. verses 1 to 10

III

The work of reconciliation

So far we have seen that the love of God, which is "unresting, unhasting, and silent as light," is at all times pressing gently upon the complex and disintegrating scheme of human affairs; that He did, as a matter of sober fact, enter once into the stream of human history as love incarnate in a human being.

He thus began by a kind of personal insertion of Himself a process of integrating men and nations which continues with increasing spiritual momentum to this day. This coming of the light into the darkness was of course no mere "flash in the pan." For wherever men accepted this human figure as the very nature of God expressed in human terms, the same love, the same power of reconciliation and reconstruction became immediately active. Christ Himself said of the man who believes in Him that "greater works . . . shall he do; because I go unto the Father" (St. John xiv. 12). There is, I think, no need to visualize what we call the Incarnation as a sudden flash of light to be succeeded thereafter by nothing but inferior reflections. It is true that Jesus called Himself "the light of the world" (St. John viii. 12), but using the identical words He also called His followers "the light of the world" (St. Matthew v. 14). And we must not through any false modesty deny the import of His promise when speaking of His faithful follower—"the works that I do shall he do also" (St. John xiv. 12).

Part of the astonishing humility of the love of God lies, not only in His human-level approach in coming down to where we are, but in His perfect readiness to use ordinary people like ourselves as channels and instruments in our day and generation in the vast sweep of His unchanging purpose. We may think it is a proper modesty on our part to assume that all work done in His Name must always be inferior in quality and effect to His own work done upon this earth. But I believe that by such thinking we are really belittling His amazing magnanimity and even cramping the operation of His Spirit, because we have not properly grasped the generosity of His purpose. "Beloved," wrote St. John, "*now are we children of God*" (1 John iii. 2). This is the kind of truth that we take as being only figuratively true, whereas I am quite certain it is nothing less than an absolute fact, far more true indeed than any "assured result" of scientific investigation. Such a high calling must simultaneously make us swell with pride and fall on our knees in humility.

We must then consider the work of reconciliation which is the initial step towards re-integration, first as begun by the unique work of Christ culminating in the Cross, and then as the work carried through by generation after generation of those who believe in Christ, until we come to our own specific work of reconciliation in our world of to-day.

In speaking of Christ's supreme act of reconciliation, we are, of course, talking of something which can never be repeated, though we know that its never-to-be-forgotten occurrence in time is a visible historical demonstration of the eternal attitude of God. And here, at the risk of appearing to contradict myself, I have to point out that this strange work of Christ is nothing that we ourselves can re-enact. We can and should reproduce the works of Christ since the power and the motive are supplied by His unchanging love, but we are in no position and never could be in a position to build the bridge of reconciliation between the holiness of God and the sinfulness of man. We shall—as we shall see presently—share to some extent in the cost of the working out of reconciliation and redemption, just as St. Paul can say that he is filling up on his part "that which is lacking of the afflictions of Christ" (Colossians i. 24). But of the strange, awe-full mystery of the Cross we can bear no part. "God was in Christ reconciling the world unto himself" (2 Corinthians v. 19). And no one but a fool would think that he could have any part or lot in that infinitely costly work.

Although this is not the occasion to expound theories of the Atonement, it is necessary to stress the *fact* of reconciliation achieved by Christ on the Cross. The theological theories of atonement, held from the days of the early Fathers to the present day, vary enormously, and probably few of us would agree in any exact defining of something which does in fact always elude definition. But we should all agree, and this is of central importance, that at the Cross we are face to face with an action that could only be initiated and carried through by God.

I have already said that Jesus Himself very rarely called men sinners, and He certainly did not attempt deliberately to arouse a sense of guilt. Nevertheless, it is universal for a human being, as he awakens on the God-ward side, to experience a sense of guilt. Almost every religion bears testimony to this world-wide sense of human failure, and there are many pathetic and desperate attempts to close the gap that man's sin has made between himself and God. In a so-called civilized country, the primitive sense of guilt and the need for reconciliation are often overlaid or even deeply buried. But those of us who deal with the problems of human souls know that sooner or later this basic need is sure to show itself. And millions have found, as they accept the supreme sacrifice of the Cross, that the haunting sense that "something ought to be done about it" is by this act miraculously set at rest. What we feel ought to be done, but what we know we could never do, we find *has been done* through this mysterious sacrifice.

At the most the human soul can only construct a desperate bridgehead towards God, but the gulf remains unspanned. But in Christ we sense intuitively, even perhaps super-rationally, that the bridge has been well and truly built and that through Him we have access to the Father (Romans v. 2, and Ephesians ii. 18, and iii. 12). Moreover, the act takes on a personal significance as the soul awakens to God. "The Son of God, who loved me, and gave himself up for me" (Galatians ii. 20), wrote St. Paul, though he would have been the first to declare that the act of reconciliation was designed to reconcile all men to God.

When we think of Christ's positive approach, does it not seem that some Christians go about their work of reconciliation with the wrong emphasis? They are convinced—and of course they are perfectly right—that the Cross of Christ is God's answer to the sin of man. They do all they can to arouse and foster a sense of sin. Consciously or unconsciously, they try to make people feel guilty, and then they consider that it is not very difficult to point them to the demonstration and means of forgiveness. I am not at all sure that this is sound psychology or sound evangelism.

It is evident from the Gospels that the appeal of Jesus Christ was an appeal to the real man who lives in each personality, covered and defended as that real self may be by pretences and disguises, to follow Him. It is a positive and not a negative appeal, and though common sense alone tells us that He realized far more deeply than we ever could how effective a barrier was man's sin between himself and God, yet He does not seek deliberately to arouse the sense of sin. Of course men felt it; of course their unreality was challenged and exposed by His reality; of course their self-love and their disguise gradually or suddenly became apparent in the light of the simplicity of His self-giving love. But His work of reconciliation began and ended in positive and active love. He knew very well that He alone could make the reconciliation between man and God, because He alone was both perfect man and perfect God. He was prepared to allow the forces of evil to close in upon Him and kill Him; He was prepared to "taste death for every man" (Hebrews ii. 9). He who knew no sin was prepared to be "made sin on our behalf" (2 Corinthians v. 21)–an experience which wrung from Him that bitter cry from the Cross, "My God, my God, why didst thou forsake me?" (St. Matthew xxvii. 46 lit.).

Yet how little did Christ advertise or even mention, even to His closest disciples, the appalling depth to which He must plunge to win men to God. It is as though love was more important than the action of love, however fearful and far-reaching in consequence the ultimate sacrifice might be. If I may use a human illustration to reflect most imperfectly my feeling on this matter: A man who has rescued his friend from death at great personal risk, does not need, nor does he feel inclined, to bring up the matter every time they meet. Or to take a further human illustration: You and I are living to-day in freedom because during the late war other men gave their lives, their health, their sight, even their sanity for our liberty. Now whether we like it or not, whether we believe it or not, or even whether we know it or not, we are free because of them. To an infinitely greater and more permanent degree the unique sacrifice of Christ has changed the relationship between man and God. Whether a man knows it and feels it or not, the first stupendous step has been irreversibly taken and the world can never be the same again since God was in Christ reconciling the world unto Himself. Men may be slow and blind, or obstinate and rebellious, but the reconciliation is potentially true already. And because of this, Jesus Christ had no need to underline man's sin, but rather to declare to them and to live out the selfless love of God.

The Cross of Christ is indeed the focal point, patent as historical fact, of the vast sweep of God's work of reconciliation, for in this central act the man with eyes to see can observe the devastating humility of God. Not only did God in the person of Christ make what C. S. Lewis calls "that tremendous dive" and become one of ourselves, but He accepted the unspeakable disgrace, the horror and the darkness, that lie behind the Cross of Calvary. Yet I must repeat that the reconciliation of the Cross is but the outcrop in human history of a vast, invisible, unforgettable purpose—the love of God—"reconciling the world unto himself, not reckoning unto them their trespasses" (2 Corinthians v. 19). Backwards in time from this unforgettable act, as well as forwards, the steady pressure of reconciliation is for ever at work. And we who are lovers and followers of Christ are commissioned with the "word of reconciliation" (2 Corinthians v. 19). Amazing as it seems, and amazing as indeed it is, we who are reconciled to God through Christ are now the living agents, the local representatives, of the celestial task of making men both reconciled and whole. "As the Father hath sent me," said Jesus to His early followers, "even so send I you" (St. John xx. 21). He makes no distinction. The reconciling, whole-making energy and purpose of love which was in Him is to be in us as well, for "as he is, even so are we in this world" (1 John iv. 17).

It is both sensible and salutary to reflect on this high calling. So often we are bogged down by consideration of our own soul's welfare, or bedevilled by the thought of our own unworthiness, that we fail to see the greatness of our calling as sons of God and ministers of reconciliation. Fortunately for us we learn by doing, even by failing, so that we have not to wait until we have reached some fantastic height of spiritual fitness before God can use us. Provided that we have accepted His act of reconciliation, and have dropped our attempts to justify ourselves, we are embarked, however imperfectly, upon the ministry of reconciliation, upon the task of making men whole. We can truthfully say, with bated breath if you like, that we are "workers together" with God (2 Corinthians vi. 1. A.V.).

It would, of course, be the height of impertinence for any man to suggest that he could bear the smallest part in "Christ's strange work" of reconciliation. That work was unique in that it could only be accomplished by God-become-Man. Yet it is true that in carrying out the work of Christ there is an inescapable cost and pain to be borne, which is in a rather different sense the price of redemption. To follow Christ does indeed mean for every man taking up "his cross daily" (St. Luke ix. 23); and the carrying of that cross is a symbol, not merely of the denial of the selfish way of living, but of a certain humble sharing of the price that must be paid in bringing truth face to face with falsehood, healing into contact with disease, wholeness to a world rebellious and awry. We are, as God's "ambassadors," not merely commissioned to proclaim the divine appeal, "be ye reconciled to God" (2 Corinthians v. 20), but cheerfully and constantly to bear our share of the cost of that work of reconciliation. In all humility we can say that, at any rate in a limited sense, God is in every true Christian "reconciling the world unto Himself."

We follow different vocations, and the particular pain and cost of our part in the work of making men whole will naturally be different too. The teacher, especially the teacher abroad, has to cope with ignorance and possibly with the darkness and dull apathy which are the fruit of centuries. There is no need for me to point out to teachers that the cost of all true teaching is a high demand upon personality of the teacher. But the very demands that good teaching makes are the measure of its value in the purpose of God, who in this particular operation of His Spirit is bringing light into darkness and order into muddle and indiscipline.

Again, the doctor and the nurse need no underlining from me of the cost of their profession. They are always in the front line of a particular battle, and since the psychological aspect of healing is coming to be recognized more and more, so it becomes less and less possible to draw a hard and fast line between the healing of the body and the healing of the whole man. Although, I believe, arguing from the innumerable works of healing of our Lord Himself, that sickness and disease are never in themselves the will of God, yet their incidence is often a sharp and salutary reminder of our mortal frailty and of our complete dependence upon the laws of the Creator. It would be an unwarrantable exaggeration to claim that the sickness of the body invariably provides a spiritual opportunity; but it is true to say that in the healing and care of the sick and diseased there is an opportunity of mediating the wholeness of Christ in a way which is peculiarly intimate and memorable.

The work of the pastor of human souls is a vocation about which I naturally know rather more. And here, if we are as Christ was, "meek and lowly in heart" (St. Matthew xi. 29) the cost is often high. To listen patiently, to use skilfully imaginative sympathy, to advise wisely—these things all carry something of the price of redemption. Those of us who try not only to sort out human muddles but to strip away misconceptions and prejudices which prevent the soul from seeing its God, know that we have a work with its own peculiar tears and toil and sweat. The preacher and the writer may seem to have an apparently easy task. At first sight it may seem that they have only to proclaim and declare, but in fact, if their words are to enter men's hearts and bear fruit, they must be the right words shaped cunningly to pass men's defences and explode silently and effectually within their minds. This means in practice turning a face of flint towards the easy cliché, the well-worn religious cant and phraseology, dear no doubt to the faithful but utterly meaningless to those outside the fold. It means learning how people are thinking and how they are feeling; it means learning with patience, imagination and ingenuity the way to pierce apathy or blank lack of understanding. I sometimes wonder what hours of prayer and thought lie behind the apparently simple and spontaneous parables of the Gospels. It is not enough for us who are preachers or writers to give an adequate performance before the eyes and ears of our fellow writers and preachers; instead we have the formidable task of reconciling the Word of truth with the thought-forms of a people estranged from God; interpreting without changing or diluting the essential Word.

These are but a few examples from our many callings, each with its particular cost. "There are diversities of gifts, but the same Spirit" (1 Corinthians xii. 4); the measureless varieties of God's wisdom are at work in them all. Doubtless there are times when we all bewail the particular pains and distresses of our calling, and even think enviously of someone else's vocation, but the plain fact is that if we are called of God to bear a part in His purpose there can be no evasion of its cost. I do not suppose a little good-tempered "moaning" is particularly offensive to God. Indeed, Christ Himself once sighed wearily: "O faithless generation, how long shall I be with you? how long shall I bear with you?" (St. Mark ix. 19). But it is of great importance, indeed it is essential to our life as Christians, that we should recognize cheerfully and realistically that no worth-while work is accomplished without patience and sacrifice; and, more important still, that we should realize with a sudden quickening of the pulses that the cost we bear is, not a kind of occupational nuisance, but the honour of sharing God's cost in bringing men to Himself and changing them from wayward human beings into sons of Himself.

Let us then be clear as to what is involved in making our vocation serve God's purpose of reconciliation. Christianity is full of joy, but it is not a joy-ride. Christ was, I believe, full of humour, but He was inescapably "a man of sorrows" (Isaiah liii. 3). It is as if we were called to be, as Mr. Churchill said in one of the darkest hours of the late world war, both grim and gay. The grimness comes from our knowledge of the strength of the forces arrayed against us: the stubbornness of human self-will, the sheer dead weight of apathy which above all else would quench the fires of our spirit. But gay we must be too, because day by day we have the deepest satisfaction this world can afford, of knowing that we are co-operating with—and even being allowed to share the cost of—the purpose of God Himself.

Of course we often feel discouraged. We think of our high calling and are dismayed at the meagre response to our labour. We see, in a kind of indelible vision, the unfailing, reconciling purpose of God, and we are surrounded by thousands who see no such thing. For all our labours, for all our heartbreaks and our pain, we have so little to show. The remedy is to "consider him" (Hebrews xii. 3), and not to lash ourselves with useless feelings of guilt, failure and frustration. Consider Him. Was He, incarnate love in person, a success? Should we, if we did not know the answer already, consider His mission successful, when at the time of crisis "all the disciples forsook him, and fled"? (St. Matthew xxvi. 56, A.V.) Are we expecting more favourable results than He achieved? Or are we prepared, as He was, to "dare to take the awful patient ways of God" and be content to do the Father's will?

We must not be infected by the world's valuations of either speed or success. The responsibilities which faced Christ as a human being would be, if we stop to think, enough to drive the most balanced man out of his mind. But He maintained His poise, His joy and His peace. He did the Father's will; and that is both the most and the highest that we can do.

IV

Inner resources for the task

Passages which should be studied in connexion with the following chapter are:

I JOHN iii. verses 1 to 10
GALATIANS iii. verses 26 to the end, and GALATIANS iv. verses 1 to 7

IV

INNER RESOURCES FOR THE TASK

AS WE GROW UP, OUR MINDS DEVELOP IN A SCORE OF DIFFERENT ways. Our experience and our insight into people, ideas, and problems grow deeper. At the same time, unless we have allowed ourselves to become bogged down by some rigidity in our religious thinking, our ideas of God expand greatly, and there come times when we realize with an awe-struck humility that what we once worshipped as God was only, so to speak, the shimmering hem of His garment. If we are foolish we cling with desperate loyalty to the limited conception of God that we have at present, but if we are wise, we "launch out into the deep" (St. Luke v. 4, A.V.), and allow every true experience of life, every touch or sight of goodness, truth and beauty, to open fresh windows upon the illimitable magnificence of God. We cannot hold too big a conception of God, but the more our hearts and minds and imaginations are used, the more astounding becomes the central fact of our faith—that so infinite a God allowed Himself to be, so to speak, scaled down to fit the narrow limits of humanity. For all His vastness and mystery, He has made Himself known in an unforgettable character by which all men can see what sort of Person it is "with whom we have to do" (Hebrews iv. 13). It is as though, having once accepted this tremendous fact, we view all that we can see or discover of the complex wisdom of God through a Christ-shaped aperture.

This much we see as our experience unfolds, and there also expands before our minds the "one increasing purpose." What may well have come to each one of us personally as an experience of Christ is seen to be a tiny part of a vast pattern and plan of redemption embracing men of every race and colour, requiring centuries for its operation in time, and having always as its source and background the timeless life of eternity.

Beneath the vast sweep of the divine plan, we who are followers of Jesus Christ see ourselves as both humble and uplifted. We are humbled because at the very most we can only play a tiny part in the great scheme of salvation; and, as our Lord once pointed out (with a smile, I imagine), when we have done all that has been commanded we can still only reflect that "we are unprofitable servants" (St. Luke xvii. 10). At the same time we are uplifted because through the incredible generosity of God we are called in our day and generation to take part in this tremendous purpose; and, more than that, are made His sons, not figuratively but actually sons of God "and joint-heirs with Christ" (Romans viii. 17).

As we look at the world with adult eyes, by far the most important thing in life plainly becomes this grand scheme of reconciliation and redemption. And for ourselves the most important thing is to be sure that we are taking our full part—whatever the vocation to which we are called—in working together with God.

Such a high and tremendous task could easily fill us with despair if it were not for the fact that God Himself "worketh in you both to will and to work, for his good pleasure" (Philippians ii. 13). We have thought already of the immensity of God outside us, of what is known technically as the transcendence of God, but what is so often lacking in present-day Christians is an adequate sense of God within us, that is, what is known technically as the immanence of God. Unhappily, in our day the Christian religion is all too often reduced to a performance to please an external God, while to the early Christians it was plainly the invasion of their lives by a new quality of life—nothing less than the life of God Himself. I believe this lack of faith in God-within-us is largely unconscious; for while we should be the first to recognize that lack of faith on man's part inhibited even the powers of Christ Himself, yet I do not think we realize that this same lack of faith in Christ-within-us prevents the operation of His power, and our proper development as sons of God. There is far too much strenuous, even hysterical, effort, and far too little quiet confidence in the Christ within us. Certainly Christians admit that they need the help of God in the tasks to which they are called, and certainly they seek it. But I have an uneasy feeling that many do not really believe that God Himself actually operates within their personalities. It is almost as though they visualize themselves, like Christian in *The Pilgrim's Progress,* as treading a dangerous and narrow path and winning the Celestial City only by the skin of their teeth. I doubt very much whether they see themselves as sons and daughters of the Most High, not merely receiving occasional help from God, but continually and without intermission indwelt by the living Spirit of God.

In the experience of St. Paul and his followers, the revolutionary thought—"the mystery which hath been hid from all ages" (Colossians i. 26)—is that God is no longer the external power and authority, but One who lives *in* them, transforming their thinking and feeling, renewing their minds, inspiring their hearts, and effectually preventing them from being conformed to this fleeting world. Such a conviction is indeed revolutionary, and we may well ask ourselves whether this revolution in thought has taken place effectually within each one of us; for so long as we do not really believe this truth in our heart of hearts, it remains a theological idea or a beautiful thought and has no noticeable effect upon our lives.

Startling results are bound to follow in human life once the truth is accepted that God actually lives in and operates through personality. In considering some of them I am not going to be unduly bothered by theological accuracy, any more than it seems to me St. Paul was concerned with Trinitarian exactitude. He talks freely of God being in people, of Christ being in people, and of the Spirit being in people, and I think it would be most unfair to his spontaneous writings to try to read back into them any theological implications in his varied usage. God is one God; and although we have evolved the doctrine of the Blessed Trinity in order to safeguard the truths that we know about God against inadequate and false conceptions, yet I am sure that when we are considering the actual fact of God living in us, to be theologically scrupulous is beside the point. We could, after all, be quite meticulous in theological expression and yet never really accept the fact that the infinite God is alive and powerful within every Christian.

I begin then by mentioning a startling sentence from St. John's first Epistle. It is this: "Whosoever is begotten of God doeth no sin because his seed abideth in him; and he cannot sin because he is begotten of God" (1 John iii. 9). As we think into it we shall find that this is an altogether staggering sentence, meaning, I am sure, that the Christian is able not to sin because God's "seed remaineth in him"; or, if we change it into modern idiom, *because God's heredity is permanently in him.* This is one of the revealed truths of God which many Christians are inclined to take with a grain of salt, thereby robbing it of any real effectiveness. I believe it to be not only true but perfectly reasonable and logical. For if we are, through Christ, sons of God, that is to say, not sons of God by courtesy title but really sons of God, there must be in us something of the heredity of God. Plainly this heredity we derive from Him is both incapable of sin and able not to sin. And it is a factor upon which we can reckon with every confidence. It is, of course, true that there are other factors within us, of which we are only too well aware and which to my mind are often unduly stressed. Indeed, I think we do ourselves and God a disservice by continually harping upon our own sinfulness. We do very much more good if we honestly believe and reckon upon our capacity, through Christ, of sinlessness. So often one has heard Christians taking an almost morbid delight in their discoveries of their own sinfulness, yet how rarely has one heard of Christians delighting in their own God-given capacity not to sin. God's heredity is in you and me, a potent and in the last resort undefeatable factor in our personalities. Just as surely as human traits of character will "come out" in our children, so surely will the likeness of Christ be exhibited in those who are God's sons through Him.

We are slow to believe this, and we tend to play it down as though it were somehow presumptuous on our part to believe that the very nature of God is in us. We may, and we should, feel unworthy of such high honour, but the whole glory and beauty of the Gospel is that it is God's free gift. There is no question here of deserving—nobody deserves this gift of God. There is no question of being worthy, for no one is worthy of such an honour. It is all part of God's amazing generosity that in order to make His vast plan of reconciliation practicable through frail and often unreliable human agents, He not only calls them sons of God, but makes them sons of God. He does not give them a mere tantalizing title; He implants a dependable heredity within them.

The continual unremitting work of the Spirit within us—if we give Him the right conditions in which to work—is to change us into becoming quite naturally, and as a matter of course, sons of God. The attractive fruits of the Spirit which St. Paul lists in Galatians v. 22–23 are real fruits. They are indeed supernaturally produced, but they are not supernatural qualities. The love, joy, peace, which St. Paul had observed in the lives of those who were open on the God-ward side are easily recognizable as human qualities, *and yet they are the very qualities of which human nature without Christ so quickly runs short.* We almost automatically assume that these are not fruits at all but accomplishments produced by strenuous labour and stern self-denial. But in fact I am convinced that they are the outward and visible signs of the indwelling of human personalities by the living Spirit of God. I have already spoken of that horrid thing, love in inverted commas, but as long as we regard the Christian religion as a performance instead of an experience we shall tend to produce, not only love, but joy, peace, long-suffering and all the rest as artificial attitudes, or at the most hot-house fruit. This again is because we impose upon ourselves standards and restrictions instead of being inwardly free and relaxed in the liberty of the Spirit. "Consider the lilies of the field, how they grow; they toil not, neither do they spin: yet I say unto you, that even Solomon in all his glory was not arrayed like one of these" (St. Matthew vi. 28–29). The spontaneous natural flower and fruit of a life open to the Spirit of God are as much to be preferred to the tense, over-anxious performance of Christian values, as the beauty of the wild flower is superior to Solomon's imposing magnificence.

All this may seem strange and even a little fantastic to us to-day, because we are infected far more than we know by the closed-system mode of thought by which we are surrounded. The world in its wisdom has learned many things through the centuries, but particularly through the last fifty years man has come to regard all the complexity of this life as a self-contained system in which "cause and effect" can be shown to be responsible for all phenomena. We know more and more of the laws which govern the cause and effect, but less and less are we inclined to believe that there can be any penetration of this closed world by anybody or anything from outside. This way of thinking has affected us far more than we realize, and consequently we are not only much slower to believe in the power of God and in these breath-taking promises and gifts in which the New Testament specializes, but our whole personalities have grown closed and insensitive on the God-ward side.

The unpleasant price we pay for this know-all attitude is, of course, for the ordinary man of the world the blankest materialism, while for the Christian, as we have seen already, it reduces a dynamic living faith to a rather wearisome performance. We need to make a really determined effort of faith to break through this crust of modern unbelief, and to recapture that New Testament attitude of mind by which God is confidently reckoned upon to provide the necessities for the new life. We can, alas, so easily reflect wistfully that "times were different then," and thus excuse ourselves from the consequence of believing in a God alive and active to-day. It is true that times were different then, but I think we can be quite certain that, although the enemies and hindrances of the early Church were different from ours, they were certainly not less. The Christian faith took root and flourished in an atmosphere almost entirely pagan, where cruelty and sexual immorality were taken for granted, where slavery and the inferiority of women were universally accepted, while superstitions, cults and contending religions, with all kinds of bogus claims, existed on every hand.

Within this pagan mess the early Christians, by the power of God within them, lived their lives as His sons. They were pioneers of the new humanity; they showed for all the world to see the fruits of the Spirit in human life. At times the opposition was almost overwhelming, as we can glimpse from St. Paul's second letter to the Corinthians, chapter iv., verses 5 to 10, A.V.:

> For we preach not ourselves, but Christ Jesus the Lord; and ourselves your servants for Jesus' sake.
>
> For God, who commanded the light to shine out of darkness, hath shined in our hearts, to give the light of the knowledge of the glory of God in the face of Jesus Christ.
>
> But we have this treasure in earthen vessels, that the excellency of the power may be of God, and not of us.
>
> We are troubled on every side, yet not distressed; we are perplexed, but not in despair; persecuted, but not forsaken; cast down, but not destroyed; always bearing about in the body the dying of the Lord Jesus, that the life also of Jesus might be made manifest in our body.

Now the reason for the significant "buts" in that passage is not the personal courage of St. Paul, as he would have been the first to point out, but the Christ who lived in him, as He does in all true Christians.

To-day we face a very different world, though to analyse even briefly the particular anti-Christian elements of our surroundings is not my purpose here. But the moment that we accept seriously, and by that I do not mean solemnly, Jesus Christ as Lord, we find both within us and without us a dead and depressing weight of opposition. It is depressing because it is not as a rule violent hostility, but a soul-destroying apathy, aptly epitomized by that truly horrifying expression "I couldn't care less." And it is within us as well, because the fog of prevailing unbelief has seeped into many Christian lives and choked their joy and confidence.

Now this is where I believe we have got to do battle, and to battle first with that refusal to believe which has resulted in the atrophy of the faith-faculty, and which has become so habitual as to be part and parcel of our lives. Looking aside for a moment from the revealed Word of God, can we not see the utter absurdity of God's expecting us little impotent human beings to live as His sons, His representatives, His ambassadors, unless He guarantees and provides constantly the power so to believe and so to behave. If Christian living is to be the instrument of God's purpose of making men whole, it must provide a supernatural quality of life; there must be an invasion of ordinary human life by God Himself. If God's plan is to have the remotest chance of success, then He must provide supernaturally joy and peace and love and courage and patience, and all the other virtues which we so deeply need. I say, "He *must,*" for that seems to me to be merely logical and sensible. And if we turn to the Epistles of the New Testament, which are the earliest Christian documents, we find plenty of evidence of this very thing—God pouring into ordinary lives those extra qualities which the sons of God need for their living. Some phrases leap at once to the mind:

Strengthened with all power, according to the might of his glory	(Colossians i. 11)
Filled unto all the fulness of God	(Ephesians iii. 19)
[Filled] with all joy and peace in believing	(Romans xv. 13)
Full of goodness, filled with all knowledge	(Romans xv. 14)
Able to withstand in the evil day	(Ephesians vi. 13)
Blameless and harmless, children of God	(Philippians ii. 15)

There are, of course, many more. But can we in all honesty say that such expressions accurately describe our own experience of the power of God within us? Of course, we know something of these qualities, and possibly we dream a little wistfully of how one day perhaps they might be true of us. I am quite convinced that they are meant to be true here and now for all those who in heart and mind are allied to the eternal purpose. It is laughable even to suggest that God has changed with the passing centuries or that His resources of spiritual power have somehow petered out, and yet *that is often exactly what our lives imply.*

Now when we begin to recover our faith in God alive within us, we cannot help being conscious of His purpose both within us and through us. The working out of that purpose is vast and varied, and besides the equipment already mentioned—adequate power for the job in hand to live as sons of God despite the outward circumstances, and spontaneously to produce those overflowing virtues which we call the fruits of the Spirit—we will consider two particular activities of God within us which are of very great importance.

The first is the ability to think and feel according to the mind of Christ, and to remain unaffected by the prevailing climate of opinion. In writing to the Romans, St. Paul once said: "Be not conformed to this world: but be ye transformed by the renewing of your mind" (Romans xii. 2, A.V.). Notice that he does not say, "transform yourselves," but allow yourselves to be transformed. The world inevitably tends to make people conform in their thinking and feeling to its habit and outlook, to its own pattern. The man who lacks inner resources and a vision of God will inevitably, sooner or later, conform to the contemporary pressures. We see it happening before our eyes. Modern materialism has already produced the mass-mind.

But to St. Paul at least there is an immensely potent factor working in the opposite direction, the moulding of man's character and outlook from within. This to him was nothing less than the ever present, ever fresh, ever new Spirit of God Himself, well able not merely to counteract the pressures of the surrounding world, but to renew and rearm in spite of it. Nor does St. Paul regard this inward power as a mere balancing force which enables a man to retain his spiritual balance and nothing more. No, it is an overwhelming victory: "we are more than conquerors through him that loved us" (Romans viii. 37). The power is far more than enough to keep a man in spiritual health; it spills over; it is the Spirit of love and power as well as of a sound mind (2 Timothy i. 7). We can be confident that St. Paul, whose experience of life was both deep and varied, knew what he was talking about here, and we can rely on his evidence of observed spiritual power in human life. Pressed as we are by an unbelieving and often apathetic world, we all need to see ourselves transformed by the renewing of our minds by the same Spirit. Do we believe that to be possible in this year of grace?

The second activity of the Spirit which seems to me to be pressing more and more upon the consciousness of Christians is His unifying purpose. To quote St. Paul again: "There can be neither Jew nor Greek, there can be neither bond nor free, there can be no male and female: for ye all are one man in Christ Jesus" (Galatians iii. 28). It is not within my special province to speak of the heightening of racial tensions on the one hand, or the breaking down of prejudices on the other. Such a subject needs expert treatment. Nor am I qualified to speak, except as an ordinary parish priest, of the deep and growing desire for unity in Christ which is expressing itself on all hands, while at the same time die-hards of various parties are putting up what we may hope are their last defences. But anyone with half an eye can see that there is beginning to emerge a new sense of common humanity on the one hand, and at the same time a steadily increasing pressure towards unity within the Church itself.

It would be fascinating to explore the possible inter-relation of these two phenomena of our day. While I have neither the knowledge nor the experience to do that, it is at least possible to surmise that both these movements are taking place under the gentle but insistent pressure of the same Spirit. I am a firm believer in what I may perhaps call the extra-mural work of God's Spirit, and it would not surprise me to find that in His passion for the wholeness of all His creatures God is bringing about, by any and every means that He may use under the limits that He has set Himself, the unity of mankind. There is a school of psychology which advances the attractive hypothesis that all men share a common unconscious mind, and that they are therefore linked in one beneath the level of what we call personality. This may or may not be true. But it is most certainly true of those who through Christ are the sons of God. At all times they are brothers; at all times they share the family likeness, and together they comprise the "one new man" which St. Paul had seen as it were in embryo. It is said to be a mark of maturity to recognize ever more fully our common humanity with our fellows, and that, I think, is true. Surely the Christian, the son of God, indwelt by God, transformed in heart and mind by the God who lives within Him, the pioneer of the new humanity, should be the first to realize what the Spirit is driving at—the making whole of all men in Christ.

V

COMPLETENESS IN CHRIST: IN TIME AND IN ETERNITY

Passages which should be studied in connexion with the following chapter are:

1 CORINTHIANS xii. verses 4 to 27
2 CORINTHIANS iv. verses 16 to the end,
and 2 CORINTHIANS v. verses 1 to 10

V

Completeness in Christ: In Time and in Eternity

In varying degree we achieve a mental and spiritual vision of the vast scale of the operation by which God intends to establish His purpose of wholeness in this disintegrated and disrupted world. From our present limited point of view this will always seem not only a slow but even an inefficient process. Once we have accepted what we believe to be factually true, and have grasped the purpose behind the Spirit's constant movement, we are tortured, or at least continually irritated, by the contrast between what we observe happening in the world and what we believe, and indeed can see in imagination, could and should happen if the rule of Christ were accepted. If we are enthusiastic, we are continually tempted to force the pace, and it is perhaps salutary to remind ourselves that although we understand to some extent the great increasing purpose, yet it will always remain somewhat mysterious, inexplicable and indeed unsatisfactory to our natural minds. This is particularly true in an age such as ours which is hag-ridden by regulations, forms, numbers, Gallup-polls, statistics and every other modern device which tries to rationalize and regularize the complex factors of human life.

There is an apparent capriciousness and arbitrariness about the working of the Spirit of God which laughs at our modern docketing. The Spirit, like the wind, said Jesus, "bloweth where it listeth" (St. John iii. 8), and though we can fulfil conditions and, so to speak, set our sails to meet the wind of the Spirit, yet (to change the metaphor) we can never harness or organize the living Spirit of God. We are indeed sure of His gentle purpose, but the details of His plan lie beyond our understanding and it is at once more sensible and more fitting for us to cultivate a sensitivity to the leading of the Spirit rather than to arrange His work for Him!

This unpredictable and supra-rational movement of the Spirit is an element in God's working which makes the whole Christian enterprise on which we are engaged at once more exciting and more difficult. "There were many widows in Israel in the days of Elijah . . . and unto none of them was Elijah sent, but only to Zarephath . . . unto a woman that was a widow," said Jesus (St. Luke iv. 25–26), and He offered no comment on the seeming arbitrariness of the Spirit's working. Those who are responsible for what nowadays we call missionary strategy have always the difficult task of keeping in touch with the tides and currents of the Spirit of God as He pursues His "immemorial plan."

Now this apparently fortuitous element in the grand work of redemption, and which incidentally can be seen on a small scale in the working of any local church in which the Spirit is operating at all, is singularly exasperating to the tidy-minded. What God works in one place or in one person ought, we feel, to work in all places and in all persons. But we are not dealing with, shall we say, an electrical circuit in which the power of electricity can always be relied upon to do the same thing under the same conditions. We are not using an impersonal force, and if there is any question of using, it is He who uses us and not we Him. God is of course really moving, with what, from His point of view, if I may say so reverently, I can only describe as celestial ingenuity. But to us, who at the most only know the superficial facts of the situation, His actions may at times appear arbitrary or even capricious. I do not think we need to go "all solemn" about this, or to over-emphasize our own ignorance and sinfulness. It is surely far better to accept with good humour the situation as it is—that His thoughts are higher than our thoughts, and His ways higher than our ways (Isaiah lv. 8–9); and to realize that though we are called to this tremendous task of co-operation with Him, and are no longer servants but friends, we still need to be most humble, teachable and flexible as we follow His leading.

Another of our human weaknesses is to expect our own experience of God to be reproduced in identical terms in the experience of another. Worse than this, we sometimes tend to think that if another's experience is not the same as ours, it must be either spurious or incomplete. Now here we must be very firm with ourselves and use our common sense as well as our charity. People themselves differ greatly in their capacities and gifts, and also in their particular inward needs. One may need to be provoked and challenged by the Spirit of God; another may need relaxation and the release of laughter by the same Spirit. One may need painful lessons to reduce pride and over-confidence; another may need tender love and encouragement by the same Spirit. We all tend to overlook the beam in our own eye to which we are so accustomed, and to magnify the mote which is in our brother's eye. Only God knows the relative size and importance of the assorted beams and motes that exist between us, and much the most sensible thing to do is to leave God to deal with each individual Christian with the infinite variety and delicacy of His own love and wisdom. If we feel we must do something about the spiritual life of another Christian, the most constructive thing we can do is to keep our hands off and our tongues quiet, and to pray.

St. Paul is very rarely amusing, but the passage in 1 Corinthians xii. about the various parts of the body is not without its humour. The idea of the human body being one huge ear, for example, or one vast eye, strikes me as not without humorous possibilities. And indeed the sense of humour, which is closely allied to the sense of proportion, is an essential part of the equipment of those who are called to work together in the service of God. The spirit which St. Paul typifies in this passage is by no means dead. For example, in his enthusiasm the evangelist often finds it difficult seriously to imagine that anyone could be called *not* to be an evangelist. The man of vision and imagination finds it difficult to see the value of those who do no more than plod on faithfully along a well-tried road. The man whose concern is personal dealing with people and leading them to understand God better finds it difficult to be patient with the theologian or the Christian philosopher whose work is in the quiet of a book-lined study. Yet the truth is that the wholeness which God is working to achieve is never complete in an individual, but through individuals living together as one body, each supplying the deficiencies of the others. I hesitate to speak of that of which I know little, but surely this is true too of differing racial characteristics. The Englishman, the African and the Indian, for example, may exhibit a certain limited wholeness in themselves and in their own church, but it is only when they learn to work together that they begin to realize a greater wholeness than they had previously imagined—the wholeness of the "one new man" in Christ.

This particular problem of wholeness may press upon the individual in different ways, according to vision, temperament and spiritual experience. What I am pleading for here is the recognition that there are three fairly well defined stages of the work of God in making men whole, though, of course, they are all very much inter-related.

The first is the stage at which a man sees himself, either instantaneously or gradually, as a personality in conflict with itself. By contact with the love of God, through which he is reconciled to His Father, he realizes his true self. By the power of God's Spirit within him, he is able to stand and grow and work as a whole man, though obviously at any given time he is far from realizing God's complete plan for him.

Then, since Christians have need not only of God but of each other, there is the stage where a man realizes his need of his fellow Christians and their need of him. Again, the process may be quick or slow, but sooner or later he realizes the truth of St. Paul's famous passage in 1 Corinthians xii, that there are "many members, yet but one body" (v. 20, A.V.). He realizes too that "there are diversities of gifts, but the same Spirit" (v. 4), and that it is only by true fellowship and co-operation with others that any kind of wholeness can come into being in the local community.

The third stage, and here the best of us are but learners, is to realize, not in theory but in practice, that in this world that God has made the various races, with their particular contributions, need one another to make the "one new man." There is no practicable way of achieving this except through the common realization of sonship through Christ. All of us who have had any experience of Christian fellowship with other races know the thrilling and heart-warming sense of unity which we thus experience; a unity which would not be possible except through a shared realization of God through Christ. Some parts of the Church are plainly far in advance of others in experiencing this enriching wholeness, but all of us have a long way to go before we see how far-reaching the plan of wholeness really is. There is a good deal of prejudice, often unconscious, to be overcome, and a good deal of blindness to be illuminated; sacrifices must be made and springs of charity unsealed, before this wholeness of mankind becomes a practical proposition. Yet there can be no doubt that it is towards this experience of wholeness that the Spirit of God is gently but remorselessly driving us all, and any step we take towards it is a step in the right direction.

These are the three stages normally experienced in comprehending the gist of the divine purpose. But there is a fourth stage, a fourth dimension, of which we have an inkling as soon as we embark upon "eternal life" in the here-and-now—the fact of what, for want of a better name, we call eternity. No follower of Christ goes on for long or far without realizing both the utter necessity as well as the grandeur of this immense back-cloth against which our brief life is set.

Our forefathers of a few generations ago, though they made many grave mistakes and had several remarkable blind spots, were for the most part conscious that they lived *sub specie aeternitatis*. They may have had crude ideas about rewards and punishments, heaven and hell, but at least they believed that this life was to be lived responsibly with an eye to future destiny. Their idea of heaven may not commend itself to us, but they certainly believed that this transitory life was but a prelude to a sharing in the bliss of life hereafter. And from that belief they derived both comfort and courage.

To-day the picture is changed indeed. In a sharp reaction from the idea that "this little life can't matter very much anyway," and that "souls are more important than bodies," a vast amount of Christian thought and action is spent upon the improvement and development of man in this temporary set-up. No harm in that, surely, you may object. Of course not; but if we swing too far we find ourselves party to a point of view which only tolerates Christianity because of its social implications; because it tends to stabilize the home, to improve health and living conditions, or to reduce the rate of juvenile delinquency. Before we know where we are we have lost the authentic, other-worldly note; we find ourselves regarding death, like any pagan, as an utter disaster; and, like any disillusioned humanist, becoming bitterly disappointed that men do not always "love the highest when they see it." The emphasis, you see, even among Christians has shifted to this world, and to a large extent we have forgotten that "we have not here an abiding city, but we seek after the city which is to come" (Hebrews xiii. 14).

In the early Church the sense of eternity being only a hand's breadth off is very strong. This was partly, of course, because its members momentarily expected the personal return of Christ, which would mean eternity breaking through into this little sin-infected world; partly because death by martyrdom was never very far from them or their friends, and this would mean not disaster but being received into the presence of Christ. And because of the overt and obvious godlessness of the surrounding world, they laid up their "treasures in heaven" (St. Matthew vi. 20), and set their minds "on the things that are above, where Christ is, seated on the right hand of God" (Colossians iii. 2). It is true that their Master had taught them to pray: "Thy kingdom come. Thy will be done, as in heaven, so on earth" (St. Matthew vi. 10), and they lived that prayer as well as prayed it. Yet they do not seem to have been unduly worried that the Kingdom might be barely established, the will done by a mere handful, before eternity, the Real Order, came breaking through in power and vindication.

Plainly, as the hope of Christ's coming faded, persecution ceased, and the Church grew rich, powerful and influential, this sense of an imminent reality in which all Christians were rooted began to lose its vividness and its urgency. Yet the sense of eternity was never altogether lost, and it is not until we come to quite modern times that we find *among Christians* an insistence on the value of God's work in this world and a rather horrifying vagueness about the real world beyond.

Christians to-day are naturally revolted by the kind of Victorian piety which could exploit the physical energies of men, women and children and then spend a small part of the proceeds in building mission-halls to save their souls! No doubt unconsciously they are reacting sharply against that kind of attitude. Yet in their passionate affirmation of the relevance of the Christian faith to the whole needs of man, spiritual, mental and physical—and heaven knows it is the only faith which is really relevant to those needs—they sometimes lose sight of the transitory nature of this present life, and the glory and magnificence of the life to come.

I should like to hear St. Paul reply to the Communist gibe:

Work all day, live on hay,
There is pie in the sky
When you die.

I am certain that to St. Paul and his contemporaries the quality of the pie in the sky is such that it honestly does not matter if you do work all day and live on hay on your way towards it! "I reckon [he says] that the sufferings of this present time are not worthy to be compared with the glory which shall be revealed to us-ward" (Romans viii. 18). To him heaven was not some shadowy compensation and reward, but a solid "weight of glory" (2 Corinthians iv. 17), no doubt indefinable in earthly terms, but none the less permanent and utterly dependable. Such a faith was certainly no "opiate of the people" to these early Christians; the certainty of being sons of eternity gave them a fire and a cutting edge which the Church has rarely equalled since.

Again, lacking the background of eternity we grow, if we are not careful, too high and mighty to think of reward. We work for the good of our fellows and we despise the "profit motive." Yet Jesus Himself quite frequently spoke both of rewards and of punishments in the real world, and did not appear to despise consideration of either. And while He exposed the folly of earthly treasure-seeking, He strongly commended laying up "treasures in heaven" (St. Matthew vi. 20), and indicated the kind of conduct of which He could predict "great is your reward in heaven" (St. Matthew v. 12). St. Paul, for all his tremendous sense of that real world to which he belonged, was not so superior that he could not write "wherefore we labour, that . . . we may be accepted of him" (2 Corinthians v. 9, A.V.). Is it because we are affected far more than we know by the prevailing scepticism of our age about the world to come that we place nearly all our emphasis upon the present?

It may well be asked what this consideration of eternity has to do with our present task of "making men whole" in the Name and power of Christ. Yet it is in fact most relevant, because without the dimension of eternity we doom ourselves to bitter disappointment and frustration, besides leaving ourselves with an altogether unmanageable burden of insoluble problems. Quite literally we take too much upon ourselves when we refuse to believe in "the ages to come" (Ephesians ii. 7). With true poetic insight Browning wrote: "On earth the broken arcs; in heaven, a perfect round." Unless we hold firmly to our rooting in eternity, we shall be left with an awkward armful of broken arcs which no ingenuity can assemble into a perfect round! The fact is that eternity is an essential part of man's existence as a son of God, and without it there is no perfect wholeness. There is neither time nor room enough in this cramped and limited life for anything but the beginnings, decisive and pregnant though they are, of Christ's tremendous work.

There is a certain pitiable absurdity about the humanist who loves his fellow men but has no belief in any life beyond the grave; and this may be a salutary object-lesson to Christians who have nothing but the vaguest belief in the reality that is to come.

Let us, the humanist says in effect, work for the good of mankind, teaching, healing, improving. We shall always be "working for posterity," but that is a fine, unselfish thing to do and we must not mind that. Very well then, let us assume that this fine work is successful and that in the remote future the human beings then living on this planet will have conquered Nature by scientific knowledge. All tensions and maladjustments of personality will have been removed by vastly improved psychological methods, and men and women will be unbelievably healthy, wealthy and wise. But what after that? This planet will eventually cease to be able to support life or will be destroyed by collision with another celestial body. This means that the sum total of human progress, of every effort and aspiration and ideal, will be annihilation in the deathly cold of inter-stellar space. *And there is nothing more to come.* Of course, if men stop short of the final scene they may persuade themselves that the eventual happiness of our descendants a million years hence is a worthy ideal for which to live and die. But if the end of it all is *nothing, sheer non-existence,* surely no one but a fool can call that an ideal worthy of his adult allegiance.

But supposing this life is the preparatory school, the experimental stage, the probationary period, the mere prelude to real living on such a wide and magnificent scale that the imagination reels at the thought of it—then what exciting hopes invade our hearts! Indeed, we already have inklings and intuitions that these things are true. "In this tabernacle [we] do groan, being burdened," wrote St. Paul (2 Corinthians v. 4); yet why in fact should we groan or feel burdened unless it is that we are born for a higher estate, destined for "the liberty of the glory of the children of God" (Romans viii. 21)? To change the metaphor, we are like deep-sea divers moving slowly and clumsily in the dim twilight of the depths, and we have our work to do. But this is not our element, and the relief of the diver in coming back to fresh air and sunlight and the sight of familiar faces is but a poor picture of the unspeakable delight with which we shall emerge from our necessary imprisonment into the loveliness and satisfaction of our true Home. It will be tears of joy as well as of sorrow that God will wipe away from our faces in that day (Revelation vii. 17).

It is against such a solid and reliable background that we are called to live as strangers and pilgrims in this evil and imperfect world. Our certainty of that background must not, of course, lead us to look upon this life as no more than a tiresome interlude, and so to fix our minds upon the heavenly vision that we fail to see and respond to the needs all around us! But I do not seriously think there is much danger of that. It is the man who is *not* certain of God, *not* certain of the vastness of God's patience, and *not* certain of the reality of eternity, who grows cynical and loses hope. What, after all, can such a man say to the one who is born blind and deaf, to the mentally deficient, to the victim of incurable disease, to the parents of an only child killed in a tragic accident?

How right was St. Paul when he wrote, "If in this life only we have hoped in Christ, we are of all men most pitiable" (1 Corinthians xv. 19). But our hope in Christ is not confined to this life; we dare not limit His work to this little temporary stage. Behind our imperfections lies His utter perfection. We see His work of "making men whole" begun, but we never see it complete. We see His Kingdom growing in size and strength, but we never see it universally established. Do we need to be reminded that as time goes on the numerical strength of that Kingdom in the unseen world outnumbers more and more the Church on earth? His Kingdom, in truth, is not of this world.

We do not know the ultimate purpose of God; the most we can do here is to see and to know "in part" (1 Corinthians xiii. 9). But we can see the out-working in time and space of a vast plan whose roots are in eternity. It is something far greater, more far-reaching, more noble, more generous than most of our forefathers could imagine. We cannot shut our eyes to the breadth and depth of that purpose. The highest, the best and the most satisfying thing that we can do is to ask to be allowed to co-operate with God's infinite patience in making men whole.

vain attempts to make the distinction, as witne... that, the more knowledge we obtain of the caus... leading back from a given action to a set of even... were clearly beyond the agent's control, the less co... dence we have in holding that he acted "freely."

Therefore, if, as seems hardly to require explicit statement, we are morally responsible for only those of our actions that are done freely, or, to put it even more conservatively, if we are not responsible for actions we cannot help doing, then it follows that nobody is morally responsible for anything.

Solutions

Even in formulations as relatively unsophisticated as the foregoing, the problem has elicited a wide variety of mutually incompatible responses from the philosophers who have dealt with it. The very notion of *causation* has been attacked as an outmoded, anthropomorphic relic of primitive thought, unfit for modern science, which is said to employ instead the concept *functional relationship*. (Whether the motion of the moon, together with other factors, causes the motion of the tides, or vice versa, is said to be an issue without real content; the important fact is that the two motions vary functionally with each other.) Or, the *notion* of causation is accepted, but it is simply denied that every event is the effect of antecedent causes, exceptions being made for human volitions and certain subsequent actions. Or, it is agreed that events, including human actions, are indeed always the effects of antecedent causes, but it is denied that these causes determine their effects with anything more than statistical probability. Or again, in a desperate attempt to make room for "free" actions, it is argued that, while the physical world is completely deterministic or nearly so, the events that constitute the realm of thought are much less rigidly connected with their mental and physical antecedents.

to which the following chapters are devoted, we should take into account the possibility that the best diagnosis of the trouble is that the fundamental concepts involved—e.g., those of truth, class, moral responsibility, and "external world"—are radically defective in the sense that, the clearer we get about them, the clearer it becomes that they lead to contradiction and must be repaired, if possible, or, failing that, replaced.

2

THE FREEDOM OF THE WILL

Like any other problem, the problem of the Freedom of the Will can be formulated in many ways.[1] In fact, the diversity of statements and associated definitions that philosophers have offered under this heading is so great that in some cases it seems more natural to say that certain ingredient terms are being used in different senses than to describe the given statements as different versions of the same problem.

I shall consider that we have before us two formulations of a single problem rather than two wholly different problems when there is a simple and obvious method that will transform any solution of either into a solution of the other. Of course it is often possible to notice that there is such a method even when one does not have in hand a solution to either version. This applies in particular to the Free Will problem, where, if I am right, nobody has found an acceptable solution to any version.

The Problem

In one of its simplest forms the problem has been presented as follows. Every event is the effect of antecedent

vents, and these in turn are caused by events a
o them, and so on, as far back in time as one ma
to go. Human actions are no exception to this
although the causes of some of them are much
understood than the causes of certain other types
it can hardly be denied that they do have causes
these causes determine their effects with the s
tainty and inevitability that are found in every o
of case. In particular, those human actions usua
free are, each of them, the ultimate and inevitabl
events occurring long before the agent was born
which he obviously had no control; and, since
not prevent the existence of the causes, it is clea
could not avoid the occurrence of the effec
sequently, despite appearances to the contrary
actions are no more free than the motion of the tic
rusting of a piece of iron that is exposed to water a

Thus if, for example, it is asked what esse
ference there is between my action in "freely
"Yes" when you talk me into a game of cards
action in saying "Ouch!" when you stamp on my
answer is: none. In one case the vocal mechanis
tuated by a relatively simple sequence of neur
leading from a violent stimulation of nerve endin
toe; in the other, the process is more complicated
ing *inter alia* a stimulation of the auditory nerves
sults from the impact upon the eardrums of conde
and rarefactions of the surrounding air. But
minimize the difference between being struck b
object and being "bombarded" with words—it
that the precise way in which the cause produces t
is not relevant here. Nor is the fact that, in gen
have a much less adequate or detailed understa
the mechanisms by which our so-called free acts
duced than of those accounting for the rest of wha
Indeed, it is this very ignorance, and not an esse
ference between the kinds of action, that encour

But far and away the most effective solution to the problem (in the simple form in which we have so far stated it) was offered by David Hume, who saw that suggestions like those in the preceding paragraph either involve ad hoc and untenable distinctions among the various kinds of events that constitute the world or in any case fail to explain why some human actions are free and others are not. Hume, whose purported solution has been repeated in its essentials and elaborated by Schlick, Russell, and other latter-day philosophers, finds that the source of the problem is confusion about the relation between liberty and necessity. He agrees that every event is the effect of antecedent causes, and he agrees that there is a necessary connection between cause and effect, but he denies that this implies that human actions are never free. On the contrary, he argues, my action is free if it is the effect of the determinations of my own will; otherwise it is not. To act freely *is* to act as I will.[3] Thus, the difference between our free acts and our other acts is not that the latter are determined by certain causal antecedents while the former are wholly or partially exempt from this sort of connection; in any given case, the crux is not *whether* there are causes but *what* those causes are. If someone's action is the effect of his own choice, it is free and he bears the moral responsibility for it; if it is the effect of someone else's choice, then he may plead that he acted under duress or compulsion and is therefore not subject to praise or blame.

Having shown, as he thinks, that the existence of human freedom and responsibility is in no way incompatible with the fact that the universal law of causation applies to human actions as strictly and completely as it applies anywhere else, Hume adds the further consideration that *only* because our actions are causally related to our motives do the former have any moral quality whatever, i.e., are properly the objects of moral approbation or the opposite. Unless actions can be affected by motives, there is no point in exhorting someone to behave himself and no justice in blaming him if he does not. Therefore, determinism, in the sense that whatever we do is causally determined by antecedent events, is not only compatible with morality, it is absolutely indispensable to it.[4]

Moritz Schlick summarizes the Humean view by declaring that the opposite of freedom is compulsion, not necessity, while the opposite of necessity is chance. Along with some other authors, he believes that an additional factor giving rise to our problem is the confusion of two senses of the word "law."[5] On the one hand, there are the laws legislated by the state; these do exert compulsion upon us and limit our freedom. In relation to science, on the other hand, the word "law" has a quite different meaning. A natural law is not a *pre*scription as to how something *should* behave but a *de*scription of how things in fact *do* behave. Although human actions, like all other events, are in every case subject to natural law, this in no way implies that they cannot also be free.

SKEPTICAL DOUBTS

I must mention at the outset that, although there are good reasons for rejecting solutions of the Humean type, there are also bad reasons. To clear the way for setting out the former, let us briefly review some of the latter. We have already noticed the patently untenable and completely ad hoc doctrine that human actions are somehow exempt from the same kinds of causal connections that characterize the rest of nature. As Hume pointed out, when we find an apparent counterexample to the principle of universal causation, we normally postulate "hidden causes," i.e., we explain the situation by saying that we don't know *what* the cause is rather than by concluding that there is *no* cause. Furthermore, this way of proceeding has frequently been proved right; for often, after further investigation, we discover the causes of occurrences that had previously seemed completely inexplicable. So there is no reason to suppose that, just because it is often difficult to find the causal antecedents for those human actions we call "free," there *are* no such antecedents. Next, to those who find the whole notion of *cause* unscientific, etc., it may be replied that, in any case, the Free Will problem can be stated just as well in terms of functional relations. For although the events constituting human actions may not be correlated with other events as simply as the motion of the tides is correlated with that of the moon, there is no reason to doubt that correlations, however complex, are there to be found by the investigator who looks long and hard enough.

One last bad reason, which unfortunately has enjoyed a certain popularity of late, is the observation that, in many if not most cases of free acts, the agent simply does not experience any identifiable antecedent episode that could be called a "volition" or an act of "willing" or of "choosing."[6] For example, I freely took a seat on the shady side of the bus; nobody made me do it; but there was no time at which I could have been caught thinking, "Let's see; if I sit *here*, I shall soon be uncomfortable from the heat, whereas if I sit *there*, etc., . . . , and so I *shall* sit there." Now there may have been some philosophers (though I doubt that Hume was among them) who believed that every voluntary free act is preceded by an introspectable act of willing, and, if there were, they were surely mistaken. Thus there may be some therapeutic value in saying that to act freely is not to act as a result of a certain kind of antecedent cause but to act *in a certain way*.

But the opposition here is surely specious. To act as a result of certain kinds of causes and to act in a certain way may well be identical. Although I had not, when I took my seat in the bus, been "deliberating" and "willing" according to the above caricature, it can hardly be doubted that I *was* in a certain characteristic state with reference to which it can be truly asserted that, *if* I had raised the question with myself, I would have had actual thoughts and feelings of the type suggested. Therefore, the no-acts-of-will observation has negligible weight as an objection to Hume's solution of the Free Will problem. He could just as well have said that an action *A* is voluntary if it is caused by an appropriate "volitional state of the agent," where by "volitional state" is meant a state of the agent in which, if he had raised the question whether he should do the act in question, he would have had the kind of inner experience that traditionally counts as a paradigm of willing.

Also, it is quite possible to exaggerate the point that for most volitional acts there are no antecedent introspectable episodes of "willing." We must not overlook the plain fact that, whatever may be the case *most* of the time, *sometimes* there *are* episodes of the kind in question. Sometimes a voluntary action of mine *is* preceded by, and in the main caused by, a temporally extended and locatable experience that can only be described as "deliberating whether or not to do so and so and finally determining to do it." Thus, contrary to what certain philosophers have recently maintained, it might on one occasion or another be *true* (and a fortiori meaningful) to say of me something like "He deliberated from 9:48 to 9:51, made his decision at approximately 9:52, and began at 9:54 to act upon it."

So much for the bad reasons for rejecting the Hume-Russell-Schlick solution. The good reason, it seems to me, is just this: in assessing whether an act was done freely, in the sense of "free" in which moral responsibility implies freedom, we take into account not only *whether* the agent willed to do that act but also *why* he willed to do it. In order for the act to be free in the relevant sense, he must have done it of his *own free will.*[7] To the extent that his willing was not free, to that extent we are disinclined to blame or praise the subsequent act. Thus, for the agent's act to be free, it does not suffice that it result from his own choice; for if he did not choose freely, the chosen course of action cannot be considered free either.

It is quite clear that in assigning praise or blame to a person for a given action we often do go beyond the question of whether he chose to act in the way he did; we are willing to consider the question of how he came to choose that course of action. Defense attorneys know that juries will be swayed, and properly so, by such pleas as: this man, who robbed the store, grew up in a poverty-ridden environment in which stealing was not only considered acceptable, it was almost a necessity for survival; all his associates did it, and anyone who declined to take part would have been considered an eccentric fool; indeed, *anybody* subjected to such an environment would probably have behaved in the very same way as this poor soul did; he was no more able to "choose the right path" than to solve a problem in higher mathematics; how, then, can society rise up in righteous indignation at what he has done?

It would be absurd, in a case like this, to say: We don't care what caused him to decide to rob that store; he did decide, and he did rob, and so he is guilty, and there's an end to it. On the contrary, we recognize that there is something drastically wrong about punishing a person for doing what anybody, in similar circumstances, would have done.

But now, if we are thoughtful, we sense the Free Will problem lurking in the background: our basic metaphysical picture of the world requires us to admit that, whenever anybody does anything, it is the case that anybody else *in those very same circumstances* would have done the same thing and that there is thus something fundamentally wrong about punishing anybody for doing anything. It looks as though the only real difference between the actions we excuse and those we see fit to punish is that in the former case we know enough about the causal background to appreciate the inevitability, whereas in the latter case our ignorance of that background allows us to say, casually and irresponsibly, "He could and should have done otherwise."

A MATTER OF DEGREE

Up to this point we have been considering actions in what is clearly a highly abstract and idealized way. We have been proceeding as though any given action may plausibly be classified as simply free or not free, praiseworthy or not praiseworthy, blameworthy or not blameworthy, whereas we know perfectly well that in the real world actions are best described as more or less free, more or less praiseworthy or blameworthy, and so on. While there is nothing wrong with employing abstractions in studying the essentials of a problem, it is no doubt wise to keep in mind the reality from which our abstractions are made. So, let us interject some examples.

Suppose that Smith and Jones are partners in a business and that Smith is carrying the week's proceeds to the bank when he is accosted by a stranger. The stranger threatens him, and Smith turns over the money. Did Smith act freely? Clearly, we already see that the answer is probably "no," but we need many more details in order to say *how much* his freedom was abridged and to what extent he was justified in handing over the cash.

So suppose that the stranger had held a loaded pistol to Smith's head and had declared convincingly, "Give me that money or I'll blow your brains out." Smith chose to comply rather than to perish on the spot, but there wasn't much freedom in that choice, and Jones could hardly blame him for what he did. (Still, it might be said that there was *some* freedom; we can imagine certain very drastic circumstances in which the opposite choice should have been made.) Now suppose that the stranger, who appeared to be of about the same size and strength as Smith, had declared, instead, "Give me that money or I'll beat you up." We are inclined to say that Smith would have had much greater freedom of choice in that sort of situation; maybe, depending upon how much the money was needed and upon many other factors, he should have fought with the fellow and tried to hang on to the money. If the threat had been merely "Give me that money or I'll make a big scene, shouting to the high heavens that you are an exploiter of the working class, trying to take your ill-gotten gains to a safe place before those whom you've bilked catch up with you," we would expect Smith to continue on his way with hardly a pause. Nobody likes a scene, so the choice was not *completely* free; but the degree of restriction on Smith's freedom would surely not have justified his turning over the partnership's money.

What these cases illustrate is the simple fact, completely obvious anyway, that the same choice may be made under varying circumstances, with varying degrees of freedom. And the varying degrees of freedom tend to induce varying degrees of praise- or blameworthiness.

Of course the degree of praise- or blameworthiness of an action will also vary with other factors besides the degree of freedom of choice. Suppose that Smith has the only available key to a certain locked building and that someone corners him and threatens to shoot him if he does not hand over the key. Under most ways of filling out this story, nobody would blame Smith very much for giving up the key. But if the threatener is a dangerous lunatic, carrying some hand grenades, and the building is filled with a number of frightened people, whom he proposes to kill and who have locked themselves in, and if Smith can see plainly that to give up the key is to doom all of these people, we have to conclude, hard as it may sound, that he has some degree of obligation to risk his own life if that would avert the disaster. So apparently the same choice, characterized by the same amount of freedom or lack of it, can be more or less praiseworthy or blameworthy under different circumstances.

However, the fact that, in the real world, freedom and

the lack of it seem to be matters of degree has surprisingly little bearing on the essentials of the philosophical problem before us. For to the extent that an action is the effect of causes beyond the agent's control, to that extent it is not free. But the greater our knowledge of the causal antecedents of his action, the more clearly we see that, ultimately, the action is *entirely* the effect of antecedent causes beyond his control, and we realize that, if only we had a sufficiently complete and detailed knowledge of the matter, we would have to recognize that, despite appearances, the amount of real freedom involved was nil. Thus, the abstraction of treating every action as free or not free *simpliciter* is in no way the source of the enigma. We therefore tip our hats to this aspect of the real world and go on to consider other elements of the problem.

How the Choice Was Caused

Let us now take a closer look at what might be called the "paradigm" situation, in which there is actually an introspectable episode of deliberating and choosing, accompanied by the feeling of spontaneity that we experience when we consider ourselves to be making a free choice. This state of the psyche, whatever its other features may be, is surely correlated with (or, as some philosophers go so far as to say, is identical with) a certain state of the central nervous system, and that state, like any state of any other physical system, is the effect of antecedent causes running indefinitely far back in time. So we need to ask: Does the nature of these antecedent causes have any bearing on whether the choice was really as free as the agent felt it to be?

The answer surely has to be "yes."

Suppose, to take again an extreme example, that the agent had been brought into the given physical and mental state by means of a drug, administered without his consent and perhaps even without his knowledge. To strengthen the example, let us suppose further that if the drug had not been administered he would definitely not have chosen as he did. In such circumstances, few would hold the agent's choice to be free, in the sense in which freedom is a necessary condition for moral responsibility. The more natural thing to say would be that he couldn't help making that choice, that he "wasn't himself" when he made it, and that, consequently, it would be wrong to hold him responsible for the effects of his decision.

Now, what are the essential features of this "not guilty" situation? Is it essential that the agent's central nervous system be altered by so direct an intervention as surgery or the administration of drugs? Hardly. For example, if the agent had been hypnotized, i.e., if the necessary changes had been made in him via his eyes and ears, there would again be no freedom and no responsibility, except insofar as it might be argued that he should not have subjected himself to the hypnotist. Again it would be said that he was therefore not responsible for the outcome. Whether the choosing was produced by a doctor or a hypnotist seems inessential; the crux is that the agent couldn't help himself, couldn't have done otherwise.

Sometimes philosophers have responded to these kinds of cases by playing a kind of semantic shell game with the word "choice." They say that, in the circumstances described above, the agent made no choice, whatever he may have thought he was doing. But that move solves nothing; our problem merely changes its verbal clothes; for when "choice" is used as we have been using it, the problem is to find some plausible criterion for distinguishing the free choices from the rest, but when the word is used in the way now suggested, the problem becomes one of finding a criterion for determining which choice-like experiences are really choices and which are not. On the former usage, the Free Will argument leads to the conclusion that there are no free choices; on the latter, to the conclusion that there are no choices at all—which seems, if anything, a little worse. So let us continue to use the word "choice" in such a way that it makes sense to say that sometimes we are directly aware that we are making a choice and that sometimes we cannot help making the choices we do.

Let us return to our poor drugged, hypnotized agent. Is it essential that he was brought to his state of mind by such drastic means instead of by persuasion? Again the answer is clearly negative. Some adversary who was much cleverer than our unfortunate fellow, and who perhaps had at his disposal the full force of an effective propaganda machine, could achieve by persuasion what the doctor and the hypnotist accomplished by more direct means. But the result would be in essence the same: to the extent that we could see clearly how the agent had been tricked into his decision, and to the extent that we were willing to say "He was overwhelmed," "He couldn't have known," "Nobody with his limitations would have chosen otherwise under those circumstances," etc., we would have to excuse him on the ground that his choice was not really free.

But must there always be a *villain* in the story, some individual who in one way or another effectively compelled the agent to choose as he did? Such a restriction would seem completely arbitrary. Even if, perhaps because of mistaken identity, he received the described treatments without anyone's intending him to have them, or even if "society" did the persuading by means of the multifarious and very effective means it has at its disposal, the agent's choice would seem to be no more free than if the compelling circumstances had been intentionally created by some diabolical individual or individuals.

CHARACTER

Perhaps we should look for a solution in the direction of "He wasn't himself."[8] It has been argued that a person acts freely if and only if he acts in accord with his own character. There are at least two ways of interpreting this proposition. In one of them it is merely an invitation to another ring-around-the-rosy game of semantics: instead of tampering with the word "choice" and defending himself by insisting that he didn't really choose that course of action, the agent now pleads, "It wasn't really I who chose." Our task then becomes one of finding a criterion for determining *who* made the choice, and the persistent Free Will problem reappears with the odd conclusion that, although there may be choosings, there are never any choosers.

In the other interpretation I have in mind, the thesis seems nontrivial but false. We say that a person's action was *in character* when, given his previous behavior and all we can infer with probability therefrom, it was just what would have been expected of him. "He vanished when he was needed; that was quite in character, for he never comes through in a pinch." "She failed to send in the letter of recommendation on time; this was very much out of character, for she is extremely conscientious about all such matters, and particularly so when the welfare of a student is concerned." Thus the question arises: could the lack of freedom in the various cases we have described be attributed not to the existence of certain causal factors but to the actions' having been out of character? But the answer to this is easy, for in our examples we made no assumptions as to whether what the agent decided to do was in agreement or disagreement with his previous patterns of behavior. Thus, in the drug example, suppose that the effect on the agent was that he chose to set out on a drive around the town at 100 m.p.h.; he was notorious for doing just that kind of thing whenever the fancy struck him, though on this particular occasion he would probably have stayed at home and read a book if the drug had not triggered his wild-driving response. I think we still have to say that his action on this occasion was not free, even though it was quite in accord with his character. On this occasion, at least, he couldn't help it. That he regularly did similar things on other occasions, that he saw nothing wrong with that kind of behavior, that in general he was very careless of the life and limb of his fellow man, seem essentially irrelevant.

Furthermore, even when an individual's actions are in accord with his character, it is relevant to ask how he came to have that character. If the action is apparently reprehensible, this question is frequently raised, with the implication that the culpability will be reduced or eliminated altogether if the "bad" character was formed by environmental circumstances completely beyond the agent's control. But the question may equally well be raised, though it will certainly seem ungracious to do so, when we are contemplating praising or rewarding someone who has behaved, dutifully, in accord with a virtuous character. Thus it is again clear that an action may not be free (in the sense in which responsibility involves freedom) even though it is done "in character."

But we are not done with this line of inquiry yet, for someone might still object that "He wasn't himself when he did that" and "His action was not in character" are by no means equivalent and that the former is the more relevant here. It might be argued that "to be oneself" involves more than merely acting in accord with the behavior pattern one has established over a period of time; it implies, in addition, acting to some extent *normally*. In other words, we might wish to allow it abstractly possible that someone might not "be himself" most of the time. Now the word "normal" usually hovers indecisively between its so-called descriptive and normative senses. Insofar as it means merely something like "average," we recognize that there is nothing contradictory about saying that the normal behavior of individuals in given circumstances is not free. However, when "normal" implies approval or positive value, we see no a priori reason why an action that is not free need be one of which we disapprove or which is somehow wrong.

So much for attempts to explicate the freedom and responsibility of an agent in terms of his character or normal behavior.

AUSTIN'S WAY

I wish now to examine a quite different idea for dealing with the Free Will problem, an idea that finds its standard expression in J. L. Austin's justly celebrated paper "A Plea for Excuses."[9] In order to bring Austin's views sharply to bear on the problem as presented above, so as to be able to say exactly where, according to him, the argument goes wrong, I shall attempt to reformulate them in my own words and style. No doubt the result will be less persuasive and far less elegant than the original version, but I hope that it preserves the essentials.

Austin's thesis, it seems to me, is that the way to resolve or remove the traditional problem of the Freedom of the Will is to get clear about the proper (and, in nonphilosophical contexts, actual) use of the adjective "free" and its cognates and synonyms. Once this clarity is achieved or even approached, we shall see that these crucial terms are abused in the usual formulation of the problem; that is, we shall see that certain sentences occurring in the puzzling argument fail in this context to make sense, i.e., to express statements.

The particular point that Austin wishes to make about "free" can be grasped more easily if we first look at an analogous case, the adjective "real." Consider the use of the qualifiers in the following examples.

1. It's a gray monkey.
2. It's a tiny monkey.
3. It's a toy monkey.
4. It's a stuffed monkey.
5. It's an imaginary monkey.
6. It's a real monkey.

Here one is inclined to say that the adjectives "gray" and "tiny" refer to characteristics of the monkey; their role is descriptive. The adjectives "toy" and "stuffed," on the other hand, do not serve to describe monkeys; rather, they indicate that (and in what way) the items before us are abnormal or *phony* and are not monkeys at all. In the case of "imaginary monkey" there is not even an item before us; this expression, perhaps, finds its use only as a component of larger expressions describing certain mental states. But what about "real"? The important point is that "real" is radically unlike "gray" and "tiny." It does not refer to a characteristic that some monkeys have and others lack, for a real monkey is just a monkey, and any monkey is a real monkey. The word "real" plays a completely nondescriptive role; we say "real monkey" instead of simply "monkey" in order to forestall the reader or listener from supposing that any of the ill-defined collection of abnormality qualifiers ("toy," "stuffed," "painted," "trick," "artificial," "freak," and so on) is to be tacitly understood. The moral is that we must not suppose that the role of an adjective is *always* to refer to some characteristic of an object that is denoted by the modified noun.

A little reflection shows that the linguistic phenomenon to which we are here calling attention is not at all rare. Even in purely descriptive discourse we often insert special words or choose one word in place of another, not to improve our description but to give the reader a clue as to how some of the rest of our terminology is to be interpreted. Consider "I entered the hall, only to find the lecturer literally standing on his head." Here "literally" is not like "ostentatiously" or "wearily"; it does not refer to a particular way in which the lecturer was standing on his head. Plainly, it serves only to assure the reader that in my statement I am not using the phrase "standing on his head" in some figurative sense. In other words, the information it gives the reader concerns my use of language, not the performance described.

And so it is, allegedly, with the word "real." As far as the objective facts are concerned, "There was a real monkey in the store window" tells us no more than "There was a monkey in the store window." What it does add is the information that we are not using "monkey" as short for "toy monkey," "stuffed monkey," and so on.[10]

And so also, according to Austin, it is with "free." "Like 'real,'" he says, "'free' is only used to rule out the suggestion of some or all of its recognized antitheses."

> "Freedom" is not a name for a characteristic of actions, but the name of a dimension in which actions are assessed. In examining all the ways in which each action may not be "free," i.e., the cases in which it will not do to say simply "X did *A*," we may hope to dispose of the problem of Freedom.[11]

To come to closer quarters with this, we must take note of another Austinian doctrine, namely, that many of the favorite terms of metaphysical philosophers, e.g., "thing," "object," "quality," "attribute," are devoid of direct objective reference. They are only what he calls *stand-ins*, or *dummies*, for certain families of words that do have such reference. The word "thing," for instance, is a stand-in for almost any noun. It works like a bound variable. "If a thing weighs more than thirty pounds, it cannot be sent by parcel post" covers "If a book (pair of boots, dog, typewriter—whatever) weighs more than thirty pounds, it cannot be sent by parcel post." "Thing," unlike a word like "dog," is not the name of a class of entities; rather, it is like "x" in "If x weighs more than thirty pounds, then x cannot be sent by parcel post."

Now "doing an action," according to Austin, is (as used by philosophers) another dummy. It is a stand-in for any, or almost any, verb with a personal subject.[12] So, if we wish to take up such a question as whether anybody ever does an action freely, we had better look at the way in which the word "freely" works when appended to the particular verbs covered by this stand-in. Thus, let us consider ordinary verbs like "eat," "sit," "kick," "shoot."

The first point that Austin makes in regard to these is, in his words: *no modification without aberration*. That is:

> The natural economy of language dictates that for the *standard* case covered by any normal verb—not, perhaps, a verb of omen such as "murder," but a verb like "eat" or "kick" or "croquet"—no modifying expression is required or even permissible. Only if we do the action named in some *special* way or circumstances, different from those in which such an act is naturally done (and of course both the normal and the abnormal differ according to what verb in particular is in question) is a modifying expression called for, or even in order. I sit in my chair, in the usual way—I am not in a daze or influenced by threats or the like: here, it will not do to say either that I sat in it intentionally or that I did not sit in it intentionally, nor yet that I sat in it automatically or from habit or what you will. It is bedtime, I am alone, I yawn: but I do not yawn involuntarily (or voluntarily!) nor yet deliberately. To yawn in any such peculiar way is not to just yawn.[13]

Thus, for any verb, there is only a limited number of modifiers that it will *ever* accept, and, in ordinary circumstances, it won't accept *any*.

A second point is the counterpart of the first: for any adverbial expression there is a limited number of verbs to which it may with good sense be attached. In particular,

> Given any adverb of excuse, such as "unwittingly" or "spontaneously" or "impulsively," it will not be found that it makes good sense to attach it to any and every verb of "action" in any and every context: indeed, it will often apply to only a comparatively narrow range of such verbs.[14]

Now the role of the adverb "freely," in any given case in which it is applicable, is to rule out the suggestion of some or all of these adverbs of excuse that would make sense *in that case.* Thus we cannot even say that "freely" *means* simply "not by accident and not unintentionally and not unwittingly and not under constraint and not..." For *which* adverbs it rules out will vary from case to case.

The upshot of all this is that the adverb "freely," as well as those other philosophic favorites, "voluntarily," "intentionally," "deliberately," and the like, is neither required nor even permissible in the *standard* cases covered by any normal verb. When it *is* permissible, in a case that is somehow special or abnormal, we find that, although we can give a general characterization of its function, i.e., to rule out the suggestion of some or all of the adverbs of excuse that would make sense in that case, there is no way of defining it in terms of those adverbs.

So, "He signed the agreement freely" makes sense in a context in which the agent might be thought to have signed the agreement under duress or perhaps by mistake; but "freely" does not describe a characteristic of his signing. It serves only to rule out the relevant antitheses. The sentence "Nothing is ever done freely," on the other hand, makes no sense; in this context the adverb can't perform its proper function, for there is no particular collection of excusing qualifiers for it to rule out.

SKEPTICISM AGAIN

Austin's account, despite its insights and plausibility, contains a number of points that are neither clear nor convincing. Some of these are relatively minor, such as his assumption that certain adjectives (e.g., "gray," "tiny") stand for "characteristics" of objects, while others (e.g., "real," "free") do not, as well as his doctrine that some general terms (e.g., "donkey," "fish") stand for kinds of things, and others (e.g., "thing," "action") are only so-called dummies or placeholders. But the place where he really goes wrong is in his principle "No modification without aberration." Consider the quotation on page 76.

The central assertion is that "Only if we do the action . . . in some *special* way or circumstances, different from those in which such an act is naturally done (and of course both the normal and the abnormal differ according to what verb in particular is in question) is a modifying expression called for, or even in order."

A closer consideration of the linguistic phenomenon upon which Austin bases this assertion will show, I think, that whether a modifying expression is "called for" or "in order" in a given instance does not depend essentially upon whether the action in question is a standard case, normal, not special; it depends rather upon what has been said previously and upon other factors affecting how the reader or listener would take the noun or verb if the modifiers were left off. The objective features of the action—whether it is normal or abnormal—are not the crux. Indeed, it is clear that in certain circumstances a modifying adverb may be called for in order to describe a perfectly normal, ordinary, standard case of the action.

Consider an example.

> For several weeks after the operation John remained in the hospital. Physically he seemed to be making a satisfactory recovery, but he was terribly discouraged and depressed, almost unconcerned whether he lived or died. He would eat nothing unless literally compelled to, and it was feared that this would lead to a gradual deterioration of his overall condition. But then, one Sunday morning, to the great surprise and relief of everyone, he ate his breakfast voluntarily, in a completely normal way, with no protesting, no gagging, no prolonged chewing. Without knowing something of the history of the case, nobody would have guessed that there ever had been the slightest difficulty in getting him to eat.

Here, in order to say that the eating was done in a normal way, we have to use qualifiers. We can't just say, "Then one morning he ate his breakfast," though that is just what he did; for the whole point is that he didn't eat it in the way he had been doing but that now, suddenly, on this occasion, the eating was once more "normal."

By the way, it will not do to reply, "But this was still *no standard, ordinary, uncomplicated* case of eating: suddenly to act 'normally' after weeks of acting abnormally is not really to act normally." Such a reply threatens to put us back on the semantic merry-go-round. Compare the following from Austin:

> I can perhaps "break a cup" voluntarily, *if* that is done, say, as an act of self-impoverishment: and I can perhaps break another one involuntarily, *if*, say, I make an involuntary movement which breaks it. Here, plainly, the two acts described each as "breaking a cup" are really very different, and the one is similar to acts typical of the "voluntary" class, the other to acts typical of the "involuntary" class.[15]

But the two acts of breaking the cup are *not* very different, and the net effect of this move is only to transform questions of whether an action is voluntary or not into more obscure questions as to what action has been performed. Similarly, John's eating on that Sunday morning *was* normal, and if we begin to individuate kinds of eating, like kinds of cup-breaking, on the basis of attendant circumstances, we shall only obfuscate matters and transform all our questions about *how* into less clear questions about *what*. It will be noted incidentally, that Austin himself (e.g., in the passage quoted on page 76, above) speaks of the *same* action as being done sometimes "naturally," sometimes "abnormally."

The essential point to be drawn from the story about John is that whether the verb "eat" calls for a qualifier depends upon what has been said earlier in the story; it does not depend upon the facts about John's eating. Even if John had been eating normally all along, but I had been telling you that he hadn't, the modifier would be "called for" if I undertook to tell you the truth about Sunday's performance. In other words, it's mainly what I've been telling you, and not what John has been doing, that determines whether, on this occasion, qualifying expressions are "called for."

The point can be generalized: the type of expression "called for" at a given place in a body of discourse depends upon many factors, prominently including what has been said up to that point and how the typical reader or listener can be expected to interpret the various possibilities that present themselves.

When we are considering these matters, it is important to respect the complexity of the relation between what a linguistic expression *means* and the conditions under which its use would be appropriate, effective, "called for." If you ask me, "What time is it?" and I reply "Caesar defeated Pompey at Pharsalus," what I have said is true (and hence meaningful), but it is a totally inappropriate answer to your question. Such a question calls for a certain kind of answer, one that is to the point, germane, relevant. Any other type of response will be perceived as odd, so much so that the questioner may well assume that he has not correctly heard what was said.

Of course, in such extreme cases nobody has difficulty in distinguishing meaningfulness from appropriateness of use. But the distinction is equally valid in cases that are less obvious, although to formulate the "rules" of conversational etiquette that we intuitively apply is not an easy task. If you ask me, "How many children do you have?" and I answer "At least three," while knowing perfectly well that I have exactly five, what I have said is true, germane, and relevant, but it is surely misleading. So perhaps one of the rules would be "Don't mislead!"; but even this would be subject to exceptions, and, anyway, it is too general to be of much use.

The crucial distinction involved here is sometimes described as that between the *semantics* and the *pragmatics* of language. But how it is described makes little difference. What is important is that it has often been neglected or blurred in philosophy, especially by the practitioners of so-called linguistic philosophy. The fact that it would be very odd to assert *P* has been taken as proof that *P* is meaningless, has no truth-value. It is no doubt rather odd for someone to assert seriously, "I cannot speak a word of English"; but the sentence is meaningful enough, since it is obviously false. Or, take G. E. Moore's old example, "He has gone out, but I don't believe it." It is quite difficult to think of circumstances in which a remark like that would be appropriate or called for, since in most cases one either believes what one says or attempts to conceal the fact that one does not. But still, if he *has* gone out, and I *don't* believe it, what I said was true, and a fortiori meaningful, no matter how odd.

Returning now to Austin's dictum about when modifying expressions are called for, we see that this is a matter of the pragmatics, not the semantics, of language. It is a question of "what we should say when" rather than one of whether, if we *did* say such and such, we would be saying something meaningful, i.e., true or false. Roughly speaking (and in matters of pragmatics we can seldom do better than that), we need to be explicit about how an action was performed if failure to be so might well leave the reader or listener supposing that it had been performed in some other way or if such failure would be a breach of rules about relevance and appositeness. Much of this, especially as regards appositeness, will depend upon what has been said previously. For example, if a question has been raised about exactly how a cow moves her jaw when chewing her cud and I am sent out to observe Bossy, it will not be appropriate for me to report back with a simple "She's chewing her cud," even though the performance is completely ordinary, with nothing special about it at all. In *this* situation the perfectly ordinary case of cud-chewing needs to be described with the help of a lot of modifiers and other devices for introducing detail—perhaps: "She's chewing by moving her lower jaw simultaneously up and down and side to side, producing a kind of circular motion, clockwise as viewed from the front." Once the question has been raised, that fact itself becomes one of the many factors determining whether some subsequent remark is appropriate, called for, or even "permissible."

With this in mind, let us look once more at Austin's examples. It may well be the case that in ordinary circumstances neither of the sentences "He yawned voluntarily" and "He did not yawn voluntarily" would be a suitable comment on the kind of yawn to which Austin refers. But this is not to say that neither of these sentences would be *true*. Further, in a philosophical or other context in which the relevant question has been raised, either of these sentences *would* be appropriate, called for, permissible. The same holds of the sentences "I sat in it intentionally" and "I did not sit in it intentionally" in the chair example.

In short, Austin's analysis does not show that in the Free Will problem the qualifiers "freely," "voluntarily," "on purpose," etc., are misused; the philosophical context in which the question "Under what conditions is an action done freely?" has been raised makes it entirely appropriate to affirm or deny "freely" in all sorts of cases that ordinarily would need no qualifiers. And, even if it didn't make it appropriate, that would have no essential bearing on the question whether "no action is ever done freely" is true or false (however odd it may be to say such a thing).

Excuses

There is a second important point to notice about the Austinian solution—and this applies to every other treatment that diagnoses the Free Will problem as arising from the misuse of certain words—namely, that unless we are informed how to carry over the purportedly crucial observations to other formulations of the problem we have received no solution at all. Even if there were something odd and unsatisfactory about the use of the words "free" and "voluntary" in the problem as ordinarily stated (in English), how would this bear upon formulations of the problem in which these words do not occur? Here I am not thinking simply of the possibility of using English synonyms or near-synonyms for the two words in question or of translating our formulation into some other language (though in this connection it should be mentioned that often the rough counterparts of "free" and "voluntary" in another language will behave quite differently from the way in which these two words behave in English). I have in mind formulations that are much more radically different.

For example, it is entirely possible (as indeed Austin himself was the first to notice) to state the problem in terms of *excuses*. Our paradoxical conclusion then becomes: the same kinds of excuse that are acceptable in certain cases could be given in all cases if sufficient information about the antecedent circumstances were known; hence, if any action is excusable, all are.

The natural habitat of excuses, as Austin puts it, consists of those situations in which "someone is said to have done something that is bad, wrong, inept, unwelcome, or in some other of the numerous possible ways untoward."[16] There are at least three ways in which the accused can try to get out of it: (1) He can flatly *deny* the whole thing ("I didn't do it, guv'nor"); (2) he can try to *justify* the action, i.e., he can admit doing it but argue that, in the circumstances, it was the right thing to do; or (3) he can offer an *excuse*, admitting that he did it and that it was wrong but not accepting full, or even any, responsibility for it.[17] Of these three types of response, the excuses are most clearly relevant to the Free Will problem.

If we are to substantiate the paradoxical conclusion that the same kinds of excuses that are acceptable in some cases can be given in all cases, we need to survey the various kinds there are. But first it is worth noting that in considering the real force of an excuse it is usually best to take it in third-person form, for there are many cases in which perfectly good excuses become rather odd or unseemly when expressed in the first person. Compare "I am insane"/"He is insane," "I was brain-washed"/"He was brain-washed," "I was poorly brought up"/"He was poorly brought up," "I cannot understand English"/"He cannot understand English." Very often it is best to let someone else do the pleading.

Now, even a rough classification of excuses is difficult to work out, in part because the most natural classes clearly overlap. But here is a first attempt:

1. He did it unintentionally, not on purpose, didn't mean to.

   He did it: by mistake (he turned off the headlights instead of the windshield wipers); by accident (his foot slipped off the brake pedal); inadvertently, through carelessness, by oversight (while reaching for the salt he inadvertently tipped over his glass); through ignorance (he didn't realize what the consequences would be).

2. He was forced, compelled.

   He was: threatened, blackmailed, cajoled, tricked, physically pushed, bumped, prodded, jabbed, etc.

3. He was powerless to prevent what happened.

   Unforeseeably: the brakes of his car failed, the wind blew his ship aground, the metal roof on which he was perched became slick.

4. He was not himself.

   At the time he was: half-asleep, exhausted, intoxicated, drugged, hypnotized, brain-washed, provoked, angered, insane.

5. He was himself, but he is not a normal person.

He is: absent-minded, poorly brought up, feeble-minded, addicted to alcohol or other drugs.

6. He should not have been allowed to do it.

   He had every reason to think that, if it was wrong, he would be prevented from doing it.

7. He is not now the same person he was then.

   It was a very long time ago; he has matured in the meantime.

Any excuse, if acceptable, removes or at least reduces the culpability of the agent for the action in question. The conditions for acceptability vary from type to type and with the particular nature and circumstances of the action, but as concerns the types most relevant to the Free Will problem, namely, types 2, 3, 4, and 5, a general feature is evident. In support of excuses of these four classes one usually sets forth, as clearly and fully as possible, the sequences of causal antecedents of the given action, tracing things back in time at least to a point before which the agent could not be expected to have intervened.

Now, an action is *excusable* if there is an acceptable excuse for it; and whether there is such an excuse depends only upon the circumstances of the action, *not* upon whether anybody *knows* that there is such an excuse. That is to say, we do not suppose that, in order for Smith's action to be excusable, somebody must be aware of the particular exculpatory circumstances; all that is required is that there *are* such circumstances, known or unknown.

Accordingly, let us for the moment try to look at the matter from the point of view of a (relatively) omniscient being who can trace out, for any human action, at least the causal network of macroscopic events leading up to that action. Such a being need only be able to analyze all physical or other relevant processes to the degree of fineness and detail that suffices in those cases in which excuses are accepted. When, through no fault of Smith's, his brakes fail and he runs into the car ahead of him, we excuse him on the basis of a causal sequence involving the laws of mechanics applied at a macroscopic level only; we do not by any means require as full an account of the situation as could be given by a trained physicist. Thus it will suffice if the hypothesized "omniscience" is limited on the whole to macroscopic events in the reasonably near vicinity of the agent whose actions we are considering.

When this omniscient being looks at the causal antecedents of any given action by Smith, either he will find in that network some volition (or choice-state or volition-state) of Smith's that is directed toward that action, or he won't. If he does not, there will be no difficulty in supporting an acceptable excuse of types 1, 2, or 3 for what Smith has done; the greater the detail in which the causal sequences leading to that act are set forth, the more convincing the excuse will be. On the other hand, if among the causal antecedents our omniscient being does find the requisite volition or state, he has only to look at the antecedents of *that,* and so on back until he reaches a time t at which no event in the network is preceded by a volition of Smith's directed to an event occurring later than t. To reach such a time, he will probably not need to go back more than a hundred years. If he then outlines the causal sequences preceding the relevant volitions he has found, he will have before him the necessary basis for an excuse of types 2, 4, or 5.

For example, Smith has injured himself by falling from a sloping metal roof on which he was hired to work. He sues the owners of the building; they argue that the accident was his own fault. Tracing out the events leading to the fall, we do, of course, find a volitional state of Smith: of his own "free will" he got up onto the roof. But this volitional state is irrelevant because it was not directed to the act in question, i.e., the fall.[18] For the rest, we find only mechanical circumstances: while Smith was on the roof, it became covered with an almost imperceptible dusting of detergent powder, emitted from the owner's adjacent soap plant; a light sprinkle of rain then reduced the coefficient of static friction almost to zero, and Smith's slide down the roof had all the inevitability and predictability of a demonstration in elementary physics. His type 3 plea, "I couldn't help it," is fully supported by the causal sequence indicated, and his responsibility would of course have been no greater if we and all other observers had been ignorant of these facts.

Situations in which excuses of type 2 are acceptable are paradigms of the kind of case in which an appropriate volitional state *is* present. Threatened with death, Smith chose without hesitation to hand over the money to the robber. So there was a choice, and the choice was causally effective in producing the act in question. But now we look at the circumstances giving rise to that choice. In a case like this one, sufficient causal factors are not far to seek, though even a relatively full account of the mechanism is still far beyond the capability of physiologists and psychologists. What is essential here, however, is not that a particular kind of causal chain produced the choice; *any* chain not involving a relevant earlier determination by Smith would make the eventual action equally excusable. If some diabolical entity had managed, by whatever operations and treatments, to bring Smith to the same state to which the robber brought him by waving a gun and uttering threats, then Smith's action would be equally excusable. Obviously, as we have emphasized before, there need not be some other person or entity who can be blamed; Smith's responsibility would be no less and no greater if his choice had been determined by a completely "natural" process involving no intervention by any wicked being whatever.

The conclusion to be drawn from all this is that no matter what the character of the causal network leading to Smith's action may be—in particular, whether or not it contains a volitional state of Smith's that is directed toward that action—it will support an excuse of one of the types 1 through 5.

We see, therefore, that in stating the Free Will problem we need not employ the words "freely" or "voluntarily" (or any of their cognates or synonyms) and that, consequently, the problem cannot be solved or dissolved simply by observations, however astute, that apply only to such words.

Moreover, the problem is not to be solved via animadversions on the uses of the word "excuse." The appearance of that word in a statement of the problem renders the statement metalinguistic, in contrast to the earlier formulation, which did not concern language but only certain features of the extralinguistic world. The excuses themselves do not in general contain the word "excuse" but are usually couched in completely ordinary, philosophically noncontroversial idioms: "He stepped on my toe"; "I slipped"; "He couldn't help it"; and so on. As long as *these* expressions are used in a proper way and are supportable by the kinds of evidence they seem to demand, the Free Will problem will be there, regardless of any features of the use of the word "excuse."

BLIND ALLEYS

Determinism

The Free Will problem has often been interpreted as an argument purporting to show that freedom is incompatible with a certain principle or doctrine called "determinism." And indeed, the formulations we have considered up to now are properly describable as attempted demonstrations that a contradiction follows from the assumption that some human actions are free, when we add to this assumption the principle that every event is the effect of antecedent events. Hence philosophers have expended a great deal of intellectual energy in attempting to solve the problem by showing that the principle of determinism, in some reasonably plausible and exact form, is false.

But the Free Will problem is a much harder nut to crack than that. Our picture of the interconnections of events in the world must be reconciled, not simply with the apparent fact that some human actions are free, but rather with the apparent fact that some are free *and some are not.* No refutation of determinism, whatever intrinsic interest it may have, will be of any use in the present connection unless it provides a way of distinguishing those human actions that are free from those that are not; no account that leaves all human actions equally undetermined will solve the problem. Unfortunately, up to now the only serious grounds that have been presented for doubting determinism are such as would "free up" all human actions equally; they are therefore essentially irrelevant to the crux of the issue with which we are concerned.

The task of getting clear about what determinism is and what bearing it has on the tenability of various scientific theories belongs properly to metaphysics and the philosophy of science. It has proved to be quite difficult, despite the fact that the underlying intuitive idea is rather easily expressed. In one form this idea is simply the so-called principle of universal causation: every event is the effect of antecedent events; or, the past completely determines the present and future; or, the state of the universe at any given time is completely determined by its state at any earlier time. Or (trying to eliminate the troublesome verb "determine"): there are general laws, not necessarily simple and not necessarily discoverable by human beings, such that the facts about any given (actual) event follow from these laws coupled with certain facts about antecedent events. Or, an ideal knower who knew all there was to know about everything in the universe at any particular time in the past would be able to predict correctly any occurrence in the future.

As the two last-mentioned formulations show with particular clarity, the principle seems always to be in danger of running aground on the shoals of triviality. What is meant by "the facts about an individual at any given time"? It would seem that one of the facts about Socrates in 400 B.C. was that he had only about one more year to live. So, of course, if you knew all the facts about Socrates in 400 B.C., you would be able to infer, even without the help of any scientific laws, that he would die in 399 B.C. On this basis, obviously, the principle becomes completely trivial.

Other difficulties arise in connection with the notion of law. On the one hand, there is no intuitive basis for supposing that the laws of nature are such as will seem to us mortals to be simple, economical, and beautiful; unless we are ready to subscribe to some quasi-Cartesian thesis that a benevolent God would not have made things difficult or otherwise unpleasant for us, we have to reckon with the possibility that in our language and notation the true or most probable story may turn out to be extremely complicated or perhaps even inexpressible. On the other hand, if, to avoid dependence on the peculiarities of our particular languages, we interpret "law" so abstractly that in effect it means merely "function," then of course there is a function such that, if you give it, as arguments, (1) the set of events occurring at any particular time t and (2) some later time t', it will give you as value the set of events occurring at that later time, t'. It is, indeed, just the function we have described. Thus, this route (and most of the variants on it that immediately spring to mind) takes us back again to triviality and vacuity.

But fortunately we can leave this topic to the philosophers of science and to those scientists for whom the doctrine of determinism has positive or negative heuristic value. For, as we have seen, to solve the Free Will problem (when it is stated in terms of causation), we would need some basis for holding that our free actions are less rigidly determined by antecedent causes than are actions that are not free. And whether determinism, however defined, is true or false would seem to have no bearing whatever on that.

While we are on the subject of determinism, however, we should take note of the fact that to their great credit a number of leading figures in the recent history of physics have been seriously concerned with the relation between their science and the important matters of ethics, especially those pertaining to human freedom. The rise of fascist and communist systems of oppression, together with the invention of nuclear weapons, gave a strong impetus to this. But the concern existed previously, for it dates at least from Max Planck's discovery of the quantum effect. Planck himself tried to solve the Free Will problem by utilizing the idea that in certain cases the observation of an object affects the state of the object in unpredictable ways. His argument, though confused and philosophically unsophisticated, is interesting.

> Our consciousness, which after all is the most immediate source of cognition, assures us that free will is supreme. Yet we are forced to ask whether human will is causally determined or not. Put in this way, the question . . . is . . . illusory, by which I mean that, taken literally, it has no exact meaning . . . The actual facts may be briefly stated as follows. From the standpoint of an ideal and all-comprehensive spirit, human will, like every material and spiritual event, is completely determined causally. Looked at subjectively, however, the will, insofar as it looks to the future, is not causally determined, because any cognition of the subject's will itself acts causally upon the will, so that any definitive cognition of a fixed causal nexus is out of the question. In other words, we might say that looked at from outside (objectively?) the will is causally determined, and

that looked at from inside (subjectively) it is free. There is here no contradiction.[19]

Part of what Planck is saying seems to be this: if, when I am in the midst of making an informed choice—and let us suppose that it is a paradigm case, in which I am consciously deliberating and taking into account such knowledge as I may have of the relevant facts—I try to include among the relevant considerations any knowledge or opinion I may have as to what is causing me to make the choice I am making, the choice itself may be altered thereby. Or, putting it in another way, suppose that I seek to gain knowledge of what actuates me when I make certain choices. I therefore set out to "watch myself" making an informed choice in some situation. (Again, for the sake of the argument, assume that it is a paradigm situation in which I am consciously deliberating and taking into account such relevant knowledge as I may have.) The problem is that any awareness I gain, or even any opinion I form, as to what is causing me to make the choice I am making becomes part of the store of items affecting the choice.

For example, I am deliberating whether to eat my dessert first and the main course of my dinner second, or the other way around. The pie looks very good, and I have never liked liver and onions anyway, and, besides, I know that, after eating the main course, I will be too sated to enjoy the pie to the full. But just as I am about to choose the pie-first, liver-second alternative, it dawns on me that a considerable part of the cause of my making this choice is undoubtedly my craving for sugar, which I must fight off if I am not to become even fatter than I already am. That awareness causes me now to choose the other alternative. Still further knowledge or opinions about what is causing me to make *this* choice might take me back to the first alternative. And so on.

I do not know whether such stories have much to do

with reality, but in any case we may grant Professor Planck that it may well be next to impossible to ascertain, on the spot and by introspection, the causes of a choice one is in the process of making. But this fact, if it is a fact, has no bearing on the Free Will problem.

The rest of Planck's argument is to the effect that, looked at from the outside, the will is completely determined causally, while, looked at from the inside, it is free (presumably because, from the inside, the attempt to find out the causes falls apart in the way indicated above); hence, says Planck, there is no contradiction. To ask *simpliciter,* "Is the will free?" has no meaning; we must ask instead, "Is the will objectively free?"—to which the answer is "no"—or "Is the will subjectively free?"—to which the answer is "yes."

But this is no solution to anything. We, the jury, trying to decide whether Smith should be punished, look at his act from the outside, find it completely determined, and, agreeing with his attorney that it couldn't be helped, let him off. Meanwhile, Smith himself, looking at the same act from the inside, finds no compelling antecedent circumstances and hence feels that his choice was completely free. So we are telling Smith, "You are not guilty," while he, poor soul, is insisting "Oh yes, I am."

Actions

The term "action," which of late has been the subject of much philosophical scrutiny and has even given rise to a new "Philosophy of ——" title for academic lectures, points to another blind alley. This term does indeed occur in the most common formulations of our problem, but not in such a way that its undeniable vagueness and associated confusions can be responsible for the paradoxical result.

One move that is sometimes made can be seen immediately to be futile. Philosophers have occasionally suggested that the very meaning of the word "action" involves the notion of responsibility. J. R. Lucas, for example, considers that, unless a person *P* is responsible for a purported action *A*, *A* is not really *P*'s action and perhaps is not an action at all.[20] He finds it a condition of something's being *P*'s action that *P* should be open to the question "Why did you do it?" Now there may be a sense of the word "action" that would justify such an analysis, but that is not the sense in which we have been using it here, nor, I believe, is it the sense in which it is most commonly used in everyday speech. What is more important, though, is that this move offers no way out of the Free Will problem. The difficulty of determining whether a given action is free remains unchanged, only now it would have to be described as a difficulty of determining whether a given occurrence is an action; and the paradoxical conclusion, "Despite appearances, there are no free actions," would simply be transformed into the equally absurd "Despite appearances, there are no actions." The supporting argument itself can be formulated *mutatis mutandis* either way.

The words "action," "act," and "agent," as used in the foregoing statements of our problem, are intended to have relatively wide (if admittedly imprecise) senses. I think of these words as derivative from the Latin verb *agere* (to do); whatever is *done* is an action; any straight and sensible answer to the question "What did he do?" will be a description of an action. As always, there are exceptions and borderline cases—e.g., the answer "Nothing" or "He did nothing," in the sense of "He did not do anything," may not *always* describe an action; but on the whole the suggested test seems to work. Thus, "What did he do?" will elicit such answers as

> He bribed the mayor.
> He repaired his tire.
> He fell off the dock.

He accidentally fired the gun.
While in a trance, he shot his dog.
He slept while the horse was stolen.

All such answers describe actions in the ordinary (albeit somewhat woolly) sense of that term.

It is true that the identity conditions for actions, including choices, are not clear. Some of the difficulties may be illustrated with reference to examples previously mentioned. Thus, in describing the robbery examples, it seemed most natural to say that the same action, namely, handing over the sack of money or deciding to hand it over, could be performed under many different circumstances. And, as a mere generality, this would perhaps be acceptable to nearly everyone. But in any particular case questions will undoubtedly arise whether this or that element is to be deemed one of the surrounding circumstances or an integral part of the action. Thus, it may seem to some that Smith's handing over the money while under threat of death is one action, while his handing it over when not so threatened would be another. Similarly, concerning the choices: should we not have said that, in the one case, Smith chose to yield the money rather than die but that, in the other cases, his choices were different, namely, to accede rather than risk injury or to do so rather than be embarrassed? Or can we say that, in all three cases, he made the same choice, viz., to hand over the money (rather than not)?

The more we delve into this topic, the more complications we find. Attempting to get free of inessential features of the use of the particular words "action" and "choice," we might retreat to the relatively fundamental verb "do," investigating the phrase "did the same thing" instead of "performed the same action" or "made the same choice." But then we see that whether this phrase is applicable or not depends as much or more upon the interests of the user as upon the objective characteristics of what has been done. For example, suppose that on March 2 Smith bribed Congressman *A* by handing him an envelope containing five $1,000 bills in return for a promise to support Smith's friend Jones for a federal appointment. And suppose that on March 10 Smith bribed Congressman *B* by handing him an envelope containing ten $500 bills in return for a similar promise. Now consider these three pairs of reports (some of which would not be true):

1. On March 2 Smith bribed a congressman.
1′. On March 10 he did it again.

2. On March 2 Smith bribed Congressman *A*.
2′. On March 10 Smith did it again.

3. On March 2 Smith gave some $1,000 bills to a congressman.
3′. On March 10 Smith did it again.

To the question whether Smith did the same thing on March 10 as he did on March 2, the answer would seem to be "yes" in relation to the first pair of reports and "no" in relation to the other two pairs. If the users of these sentences are primarily interested in the bribery of congressmen, the answer will be "yes"; if they are interested in Smith's relation to Congressman *A*, the answer will be "no," and, if they are a couple of detectives interested in the denominations of the bills that Smith is using, the answer will again be "no." In short, "did it" in 1′, 2′, and 3′ seems to function simply as short for the predicate of the preceding sentence; in these contexts the word "it" apparently has no existential or even quasi-existential import. For, while it follows from "I bought a sandwich, and she ate it" that there *was* something that I bought and she ate, from 1 and 1′ it does not clearly follow (in view of the other pairs) that there is or was something that Smith did on March 2 and did again on March 10; i.e., it does not follow that Smith did the same thing on those two occasions.

In view of these sorts of difficulties, we are indeed fortunate that the whole matter of identity criteria for doings, actions, or choices seems to have no essential bearing on the Free Will problem or on any purported solution of it that is worth serious consideration. Thus, any notion that we are going to get some leverage on this problem by constructing a "theory of action" is a blind alley.

SUMMARY

When all is said and done, it appears that, from among the many formulations of the Free Will problem, it is possible to distill an essence that survives all attempts at solution.

Note first that the relation of cause and effect is such that the events causing a given event *E* form a branching tree, extending upward indefinitely in time, with *E* at the base. We do not necessarily suppose that, for each event in the tree, there are "immediate causes" that precede it by some minimum amount of time, but we do suppose that at any given time *t*, antecedent to the time of event *E*, there is a "cross-section" of the tree consisting of all the events that occur at the time *t* and are causally antecedent to *E*.

Then the essence of the Free Will puzzle is this:

1. Every event, human actions not excluded, is caused by antecedent events.
2. If the causal tree for *X* contains a cross-section consisting exclusively of events that are not within *A*'s power and are not causally preceded by events within *A*'s power, then *X* is not a free act of *A*.
3. The causal tree for any act of *A* will contain a cross-section antecedent to *A*'s birth date.
4. No event antecedent to *A*'s birth date is within *A*'s power.
5. Therefore, *X* is not a free act of *A*.

So there is the paradoxical conclusion. We are inclined to reply that we have all had immediate experience of the difference between acts that are free and acts that are not;

that the very meaning of the word "free" is learned by means of these immediately experienced free acts as paradigms; and that our whole conception of just rewards and punishments presupposes a distinction between what is done freely and what is not done freely. In short, we are inclined to insist, even in the face of the paradox, that *of course* we know well enough what "free" means and that *of course* some human actions are free (hence liable to praise and blame) and some are not.

Needless to say, all of the statements, 1 through 5, like any body of discourse, involve assumptions that can be questioned and terms that are not crystal clear as they stand. But I am convinced that the assumptions can be defended and the terms explicated to whatever extent may be necessary for countering any attack upon the argument.

To *show* that a given act *X* of an agent *A* is not free, it is obviously not necessary to exhibit the entire causal tree back to *A*'s birth date or to demonstrate the existence of a cross-section of the required type. Such existence or the lack of it is, after all, a matter of fact, concerning which only probability can be expected. Thus, in general it suffices to trace out a portion of the tree, going back to a time at which the cross-section probably does not contain any events that were in *A*'s power or were effects of earlier events in *A*'s power. If that is not true of the first cross-section we choose, we have only to go back to earlier ones until, inevitably, we come to one that satisfies the stated condition. For example, if, when we are arguing that Smith should be let off because he was in a drug-induced delirium when he did the deed, it is countered that, after all, he *chose* to take the drugs and so is responsible to *that* extent at least, we have only to go further back, to a point where the causes of his choice are located. And this sort of move, it seems, is in principle always possible and is even practicable if we know enough.

So much for the Freedom of the Will.

3

OUR KNOWLEDGE OF THE EXTERNAL WORLD

Just as, in the field of philosophical ethics, the Free Will problem is surely *the* classical problem, so the problem of Our Knowledge of the External World deserves a similar status in epistemology. Both problems, in their modern or explicit formulations, date no earlier than the seventeenth century, but the skeptical doubts that constitute their foundation go back to antiquity.

The question before us here is: How can I have knowledge of anything other than my own present perceptions, i.e., other than the immediate contents of my experience? And the paradoxical conclusion, to which some very plausible premises lead, is that such knowledge is impossible.

The External World problem, as would be expected, has many variant formulations and begets a number of derivative problems that are troublesome enough in their own right. Like the Free Will problem and the logical antinomies, it has of course been turned on all sides by its analyzers and would-be solvers and dissolvers; every joint in every form of it has been pronounced a nonsequitur by somebody; every crucial term that appears in it has been declared stretched or in some other way abused or misused; and a criterion of meaning has been invented according to which the central question and its possible answers turn out to be nonsensical or at least "devoid of cognitive content." Yet, despite all the attacks, death notices, and even obituaries, the problem is still with us.

Berkeley and Hume

In the first few sections of his *Principles of Human Knowledge,* the philosopher Berkeley sets forth with clarity and force the essential elements of the skeptical argument with which we are here concerned. Focusing on the particular question of whether we can have knowledge of "external bodies," i.e., of material objects existing independently of the mind, he begins in section 3 with this observation:

> That neither our thoughts, nor passions, nor ideas formed by the imagination exist without the mind is what everybody will allow. And to me it seems no less evident that the various sensations or ideas imprinted on the sense, however blended or combined together (that is, whatever objects they compose) cannot exist otherwise than in a mind perceiving them.[1]

To this he adds the near tautology that, after all, we never immediately perceive anything other than our own ideas or sensations. Then follows the crux:

> But, though it were possible that solid, figured, movable substances may exist without the mind, corresponding to the ideas we have of bodies, yet how is it possible for us to know this? Either we must know it by sense or by reason. As for our senses, by them we have the knowledge only of our sensations, ideas, or those things that are immediately perceived by sense, call them what you will; but they do not inform us that things exist without the mind, or unperceived, like to those which are perceived. This the materialists themselves acknowledge. It remains therefore that if we have any knowledge at all of external things, it must be

> by reason, inferring their existence from what is immediately perceived by sense. But what reason can induce us to believe the existence of bodies without the mind, from what we perceive, since the very patrons of matter themselves do not pretend there is any necessary connection betwixt them and our ideas? I say it is granted on all hands (and what happens in dreams, frenzies, and the like, puts it beyond dispute) that it is possible we might be affected with all the ideas we have now, though no bodies existed without resembling them. Hence it is evident the supposition of external bodies is not necessary for the producing our ideas; since it is granted they are produced sometimes, and might possibly be produced always, in the same order we see them in at present, without their concurrence.[2]

Two sections later he sums this up by saying:

> In short, if there were external bodies, it is impossible we should ever come to know it; and if there were not, we might have the very same reasons to think there were that we have now.

Let us apply these considerations to a particular example, choosing one of those "moderate-sized specimens of dry goods" (Austin) with which epistemologists are supposed to be obsessed. When I look at the table in front of me, what I directly see (i.e., my sensation, perception, sense datum, idea imprinted on the sense, or, as Berkeley says, *call it what you will*) is, according to the received account, the effect of a branched tree of physical causes, including reflection of light from the surface of the object, passage of the reflected light through the intervening media to the retinas of my eyes, and transmission of resulting signals along the optic nerves to the brain. On the basis of what I see, I ascribe properties to the object that presumably gave rise to this perception; I say that the table or its surface is beige in color, shiny, rectangular in shape, cluttered with books and papers.

But now, as Berkeley points out, it also follows from the

received account that I *could* have had that very same perception, or at least one qualitatively indistinguishable from it, even if there were no such material external table. Consequently, if I *infer* the existence and nature of the table from what I am seeing at a given time, I am making a leap that logic will not justify. Further, the case is not essentially altered if other senses are brought into play; by rapping on the table I do not establish that the prior visual perception was in any way veridical, for (however unlikely we may deem it to be) the auditory and tactual data, too, *could* occur even if no "external" table were there at all. (I say "external table," for we might decide to follow Berkeley and use the unmodified term "table" just to refer to what we immediately see, feel, etc., when we are said to be perceiving the table.) Any single one of my perceptions, or all of them together, could be just as they are even if the posited external object had properties quite other than I judge it to have and even if it did not exist at all.

Generalizing, Berkeley concludes that, according to the received account of how our perceptions give us information about the nature and existence of the external objects that purportedly cause them, we *could* have all the same perceptions even if there were no such objects; and he adds that, consequently, assuming only that our perceptions remained the same in quality and order as they are now, we would have all the reasons we now have for believing in the existence of those objects even if in fact that belief was entirely false.[4]

Some of Berkeley's recent critics have been confused by the fact that his argument seems to presuppose the very account of perception that it attacks. This confusion is caused by a failure to understand the structure of his reasoning. He is saying to his opponents: Look here. According to your own account of the mechanism of perception, it is impossible to know that that account is true, and, further, your account implies that, even if it weren't true, you could have all the same reasons for believing it that you do now. This amounts to a demonstration that it is impossible to know that the received account *(R)* is true. For if *R* implies that *R* is not known to be true, we have the result that, if *R is* known to be true, then *R is not* known to be true. Hence *R* is not known to be true; and, since this has now been proved without using any factual premises, we can conclude that it is *impossible* that *R* be known to be true.

Berkeley's argumentation must not be taken to show that certain entities have the interesting property of being *unknowable*. His view is rather that, when we ask the proponents of so-called external bodies how they know that there are such things, we get an account that implies that they do not know this. The reason, I think is that their definitions of "external bodies" are incoherent and hence not satisfiable by anything.

These skeptical elements in Berkeley's philosophy were further developed by Hume, who points out that not only do my impressions and ideas give me no rational basis for concluding the existence of independently existing material objects; they are equally inconclusive as regards the mind itself, insofar as the mind is supposed to be something over and above the experience it "has." Furthermore, I must apply the same doubts to any of my own experiences that are not in the immediate present.[5] Thus it would seem at least abstractly possible for someone to come into existence, at a given moment, replete with a full complement of memory experiences purporting to attest the existence of prior experiences even though, by hypothesis, there were no such prior experiences. (Perhaps this is just an unnecessarily fanciful way of stating the completely obvious fact that any or all of my memories could be mistaken.) Therefore, from the fact that my present experiences are as they are, I cannot soundly infer anything about the nature of my past experiences or even that there *were* any such past experiences. Adapting Berkeley's argument to this case, we may say that, even if I had had no past experiences at all, I would have every reason that I now have for believing in the existence of such past experiences, provided that all my present experiences remained the same. Our skepticism has thus been extended to everything beyond our experiences of the present moment.

THE PROBLEM

From these Berkeleyan and Humean doctrines we may obtain a typical brief formulation of the External World problem:

> Ultimately the only basis I can have for a claim to know that there exists something other than my own perceptions is in the nature of those very perceptions. But they could be just as they are even if there did not exist anything else. Ergo, I have no basis for the knowledge-claim in question.

To this, several glosses should be added at once:

1. A stronger formulation (or a formulation of a stronger problem) is obtainable by replacing "my own perceptions" by "my own perceptions of the present moment."

2. "Ultimately." I might first try to support such a knowledge-claim by reference to what other people tell me or what I read in books, but then the question arises as to how I know that this sort of testimony is true. Answers to this question will themselves be open to further "How do you know?" questions, and so on until my assertions are either logical truths or descriptions of the immediate contents of my own experience.

3. "My own perceptions." I can either explicate "my own perceptions" in Moritz Schlick's manner as "perceptions associated with perceptions of this body"[6] or, better, I can forget about the concept "own" and simply indicate for myself, with the demonstrative "these," the perceptions in question. (After all, when I wish to notice some

feature of a pain that I have, no special difficulty arises concerning which pain is to be considered.) Thus, I can formulate the crucial question for myself as follows: How do I know that there is anything other than *these* perceptions? (The reader will understand, I trust, that the possibility he is being asked to entertain is not the possibility that only *my* perceptions exist but, rather, the possibility that only *his* exist!)

4. "Nature" refers to the quality, order, and any other immediately ascertainable features of the perceptions. It does not refer, e.g., to such a feature as "preceding by six hours a perception of an earthquake."

5. "Could" refers to logical, or maybe even physical, possibility. The futile move that goes "Well, maybe you could have those visual perceptions even if there weren't the red apple out there that you think you're seeing, but you couldn't have them if there were *nothing*—not even your brain—out there" leads to the equally paradoxical result that the only "external" statements I can support on the basis of what I see, hear, touch, taste, etc., concern my own central nervous system.

6. "Ergo." By the very meaning of the word "know" it seems inconsistent to say "I know that *S* is true, because *T* is true; however, *T* could perfectly well be true even if *S* were not true."[7] Relevant here is Berkeley's observation that if only my perceptions remained the same in order and quality I would have all the reasons I now have for believing in the existence of an external world, even if that belief were false. Notice that his point continues to hold when the term "reasons" is taken in a wide sense, to include inductive reasons or evidence as well as reasons from which the conclusion follows with logical necessity.

7. Finally, note that, to remove the apparently essential dependence on some form of empiricism, we could reformulate the problem as follows: First we define the family *F* of those sentences that purport to describe perceptible

properties of physical objects presently perceived by the speaker, e.g., sentences like

> The tomato on the table in front of me is red.
> The Transamerica Pyramid is only partially visible through the fog.
> This knife is very sharp.

Then the problem becomes: Knowledge-claims of the form "I know that *p*," where "*p*" is replaced by a sentence from the family *F*, are usually based on the nature of the speaker's perceptions; but in each case those perceptions could be just as they are even if the sentence in question were false; ergo, such knowledge-claims are usually without foundation.

SURFACES

There is a certain "argument" that often appears as a component of the general skeptical arguments we have been considering and that (in my opinion, at least) is usually misunderstood. It is concerned with visual perception in particular, although it could be modified to apply to the other senses as well, and it goes as follows.

In situations that we would ordinarily describe by reporting that we are seeing a physical object (e.g., a book, a chair, a house, a tomato), what we actually *see*, strictly speaking, is only part of the surface of the object in question. We do not see, in this strict sense of the term, the far side of the tomato, or the inside, or perhaps even all of the near side; but we infer, assume, or presume, on the basis of what we actually do see, that the rest of the tomato is there and that we are not looking at a mere portion of the skin of a tomato. Now, whenever there is this kind of inference, assumption, or presumption, there is always the bare possibility of a mistake; and if each perceptual situation is thus open to mistake, so are all of them together. Indeed, for all we really *know,* the visible world consists exclusively of surfaces with no "insides," as it were. Of course, when we look at the tomato, our visual impression is accompanied by a certain feeling of confidence, no doubt derived from the past correlation of such impressions with various kinds of impressions of solidity derived from all five senses. But knowledge is one thing, and feelings of confidence are another.

The more general skeptical argument then goes on to establish that we don't even know that we are seeing the surfaces of physical objects, let alone the whole objects; for we could have had the very same visual experiences even if there were no such surfaces.

Attacks on this Surfaces argument have usually missed the mark. First, there is the mistaken logic of those who note that the final skeptical conclusion (that there is no reason to believe in the existence of surfaces of physical objects, let alone the existence of the objects themselves) is incompatible with a premise of the argument about surfaces (viz., that in visual perception we perceive only surfaces), and who think that the general skeptical argument thus kicks away one of its own underpinnings. Such objectors need to recall a perfectly valid mode of inference used by sound reasoners ever since Euclid, if not earlier: establish not-*P* by deducing it from *P*.

Second, there is the complaint that "You can be mistaken on all occasions" does not follow from "You can be mistaken on any particular occasion," any more than "I can eat all the apples in this barrel" follows from "I can eat any apple in this barrel." But the mistakes we are speaking about, unlike the eatings of apples, are independent of one another; you don't have to be right in some perceptual judgments in order to be wrong in others, and being wrong in one case in no way makes it more difficult to be wrong in the next case.

But the most important way in which attacks on the

Surfaces argument have missed the point is that they have misunderstood the role of this "argument" in the general skeptical argument as a whole. That role is more psychological than logical. By being made to reflect that, even in paradigm situations in which he would report, e.g., "I see a tomato," what he actually sees (in any sense of "see" that might imply the existence of what is seen) is only part of the surface of the object, the reader becomes aware of the presence of an inferential (and hence fallible) element in the most ordinary judgments of perception. He is shown that he doesn't really know quite as much as he thought he did; his confidence is shaken, and he is "softened up" for the main skeptical argument that follows. When, like G. E. Moore, he says in effect that he *knows* that hands exist because he has *seen* one, he is reminded that —even apart from genuinely skeptical considerations—the most he has seen, probably, is the surfaces of hands, and that the surface of a hand and the hand itself are presumably by no means one and the same.

Thus the role of the Surfaces argument, it seems to me, is to make us a little more cautious in our "I know it because I've seen it" judgments. It points out to the dogmatist, who was planning to attack the general skeptical argument by picking at terms like "sense data," "perceptions," "percepts," etc., that, even without these notions, there is justification for more skepticism than he is accustomed to allow. He may think he can get away with denying the meaningfulness of these terms and may argue that the skeptic goes wrong from the moment he introduces them into his vocabulary, but he can hardly give a similar treatment to the word "surface." He has to admit that the implication between "I see part of the surface of a tomato" and "I see a tomato" is at most one-way. Thus he may realize that he may be confidently asserting the latter when only the former is really justified, and this should soften him up for the knockout blows to come.

Probability

Before going further, let us notice a seemingly promising (but actually disappointing) idea for extricating ourselves from the net. In reference to the table example someone may say that, even granting that I cannot deduce by pure logic the existence of the table from the nature of what I see, yet I *can* infer it *with probability*. The more visual, tactual, auditory, and other evidence I get, the greater seems the probability that there is a real table there and that I am not just having a hallucination or some other deceptive experience. So, although I can perhaps never know with absolute certainty that something besides my own immediate perceptions exists, I *can* know this with very high probability—and that, after all, is good enough. Scientists will hardly be shocked to be told that even the most secure of their laws and principles are only probable, for in their more sober moments they never claim more for them anyway.

It will be convenient to consider this idea in relation to another example, namely, the notorious problem of Other Minds (which is obviously a close relative of our External World problem). How can I possibly know that there are any minds besides my own (let us forget, for the moment, what Hume has done to my own!), and, even if there are, how can I know what is taking place in them? Surely, when I make judgments about what someone thinks or how he feels, I base these judgments on how he looks and acts; but, as we have seen, there is no necessary connection between his appearance and how he is in reality. Yes, says our new idea, but there is a *probable* connection; when he looks and acts in a certain way, we can conclude that he is *probably* angry, *probably* sad, or *probably* wishing that he were somewhere else.

If this needs to be made more vivid, suppose that I am standing next to you at the hotel's registration desk; I hear the clerk telling you, in a nasty tone of voice, "I am sorry, but we have no record of your reservation; the hotel is full, and so you'll simply have to go elsewhere." Already it seems that I can infer, with some considerable probability, that you are becoming angry. Then I notice an increasing redness in your neck and face, a clenching of the jaw, and a general look of agitation. Does this not increase the probability? Soon I hear you shouting, "This is an absolute outrage! I made this reservation months ago; I paid for the room in advance; I have a receipt. I demand to see the manager!" It is becoming pretty obvious, to say the least, that you are angry. The clerk replies haughtily, "The manager is not available. Please step aside so that I can wait on the next gentleman." At this, you lean over the counter and, seizing him by the throat, growl: "I'll see the manager, whether he is 'available' or not!" Am I still supposed to doubt that you are angry? It would seem that, even in the most skeptical, scientifically cautious frame of mind that I can reasonably adopt, I must agree that the probability is very, very high that you are experiencing that distinctive inner feeling to which we apply the word "anger." And most people, including most philosophers, would regard it as preposterous to suggest that in these circumstances I do not *know* that you are angry.

But the position of the skeptic is hardly touched by all this rhetoric. Let it be remembered that what I am trying to conclude is that you have that very feeling I call "anger"; I am not content to redefine the word in such a way that to be angry *is* to have a red and perspiring face, to be saying the kinds of things you are saying, and to be acting in the way that angry people usually act. No, let's face it: to be angry is to have that characteristic feeling, no matter how you look, what you say, or how you behave. The problem is not to be solved by merely redefining a word.

Consider now the proposed way out via probability. In support of the claim that, e.g., your being red in the face increases the probability that you are in fact angry, it will be pointed out that on other occasions these two features have quite regularly been found conjoined. When people look like that, they *usually* are found to be angry—not *always*, perhaps, so that the probability is somewhat less than 1, but *usually*. Similarly, when people have said the kinds of things you said to that clerk, especially in that sort of context (not on the stage, nor during an elocution lesson, nor in any other such special circumstance), they have almost always been angry. On this basis, therefore, it would seem legitimate to infer that in the present instance all these observable features are accompanied by that distinctive inner state called "anger."

But such a line of argument begs the very question that the skeptic raises. What has been observed in the past is not a more or less constant conjunction between redness of face and the feeling of anger but only a conjunction between the observed redness and other observed traits (such as what the individual says and does) that are similarly assumed to betoken the feeling. But that assumed betokening is precisely what the skeptic is challenging. And the case is exactly similar with the more general problem. There can have been no observed constant conjunction between our perceptions and the independently existing external objects that are supposed to cause them. Of course nobody doubts (at least, not at this stage) that we do indeed observe regularities in the sequence of our immediate perceptions and that in the conduct of daily life we greatly depend upon them; but such regularities give us no basis whatever for drawing conclusions, whether necessary or probable, as to the nature and existence of anything beyond those perceptions.

Thus, the hoped-for way out via probability has turned out to be a blind alley, and we are back to the main problem. On the one hand, it seems clear that ultimately the only possible basis we can have for knowledge-claims about the external world lies in the nature of our own perceptions; yet it seems equally clear that there can be no connection, necessary or probable, between these perceptions and the external world they are supposed to represent. So the conclusion is that knowledge of the external world is impossible. But, on the other hand, are we to dismiss as false or nonsensical the received account of the way in which our perceptions are caused by that very same external world? And must we not say, with Austin, that *of course* I sometimes know that another person is angry or sad, and *of course* I usually know that what I see around me is not just a collection of my own private perceptions?[8] Or, with Quine:

> We cannot significantly question the reality of the external world, or deny that there is evidence of external objects in the testimony of our senses; for, to do so is simply to dissociate the terms "reality" and "evidence" from the very applications which originally did most to invest those terms with whatever intelligibility they may have for us.[9]

Solutions

The responses of noted philosophers to the elements of this conundrum have been as implausible as they are varied. Once again we have that characteristic pattern in which almost everybody agrees that *something* is wrong with the argument but almost nobody agrees as to *what* is wrong.

Plato's way out is to deny that there can be any knowledge of, or any knowledge based upon, the "world of sights and sounds."[10] For him, the only objects of knowledge are certain abstract entities, the Ideas, that are eternal, unchanging, and, above all, not perceptible by the senses. To be sure, the geometer, studying his abstract figures, may find it helpful to look at rough drawings or models, but essentially the role of these perceptible items is only to beguile his body and keep it from distracting his mind from contemplation of the true objects of geometrical knowledge. In general, in our search for knowledge we may find the world of sights and sounds to be stimulating or in some other way psychologically effective, but our knowledge never concerns *it,* nor are its shifting features in any sense *evidence* for what we know.

Alas, it is not easy to swallow such a story. There is no more reason to believe in Plato's Ideas than in any other member of that great legion of gods, demons, spirits, ghosts, and other supernatural entities invented through the ages by the superstitious mind of man. The plain fact is that, if we maintain what Russell has called "a healthy sense of reality," we shall have to admit that Plato's story, if it has any cognitive content at all, is interesting as a myth but just plain false as a description of the way things are.

Descartes's solution inspires even less confidence. It comes down to the claim that God, who is in essence good, wouldn't let us be deceived, at least not on such a large scale as our skeptical doubts have suggested. When I look at the table in front of me, I certainly feel that what I am seeing represents more or less accurately a real table that is "out there" and independent of my perceiving it; and for God to allow me and the rest of mankind always to be mistaken in making such judgments would allegedly be incongruous with his goodness. But what plausibility is there in *this* story? Even waiving the question of God's existence, what assurance is there that he is not teaching all of us a lesson in humility, perhaps planning to reveal to us in the hereafter that our stupidly confident belief in an external world was actually sheer delusion?

And then there is Kant, with his way out that postulates a "thing-in-itself," of which we can have no knowledge. This comes perilously close to accounting for the phenomena by postulating that they are all due to the activity of a benevolent demon—a demon who, however, has the interesting property of completely vanishing whenever anybody looks for him. Doctrines to the effect that there are unknowable entities are very popular for some reason or other (perhaps because they help us to deflate the know-it-alls), but without exception they seem based on the obviously fallacious inference from "*X* cannot be known" to "There is something that is *X* and cannot be known"—e.g., from "What cannot be understood cannot be known" to "There is something that cannot be understood and cannot be known." One is reminded of the absurd Heideggerian move from the plausible assertion that "Nothing is the special subject matter of philosophy" to the nonsensical questions "What is this nothing?" and "What does it do?" As if one should move from "Nobody killed Smith" to "Who is this nobody?" and "Where does he live?" Just when you think that you've gotten rid of Smith's murderer and the special subject matter of philosophy and all the unknowable causes of our perceptions, you are surprised to find that an investigation into the attributes of these nonentities is now proposed.

Consider next the so-called Subjective Idealists. These, recognizing the strength of the argument that we cannot know whether there is an external world, add a bit of skepticism and conclude that no such world exists. In the words of Berkeley:

> Some truths there are so near and obvious to the mind that a man need only open his eyes to see them. Such I take this important one to be, to wit, that all the choir of heaven and furniture of the earth, in a word, all those bodies which compose the mighty frame of the world, have not any subsistence without a mind—that their *being* is to be perceived or known, that, consequently, so long as they are not perceived by me or do not exist in my mind or that of any other created spirit, they must either have no existence at all or else subsist in the mind of some eternal spirit—it being perfectly unintelligible, and involving all the ab-

> surdity of abstraction, to attribute to any single part of them an existence independent of a spirit.[11]

Or, as Schopenhauer said, "The world is my idea." Philosophers of this persuasion embrace, in effect, one half of the antinomy only, thereby leaving themselves open to scornful attacks and ridicule by those who rehearse the plausible arguments for the other side. Can the idealists really believe that nothing exists besides themselves? That if there had been no human beings, there would have been no earth, no sun, no stars? If all the choir of heaven and furniture of the earth they see around them are not to be called "external," upon what paradigms did they learn the use of that word? And do they not, by their very actions, reveal in countless ways that they have as much belief in an external world as anyone else does?

The true skeptic, however, finds that the Subjective Idealists do not go far enough. As Hume saw, the same skeptical argument that undermines knowledge-claims about an external world also does the same for the mind (considered as something other than the sequence of impressions and ideas that it is supposed to "have"), and, more than that, it applies to all past and future experiences. For what I call "remembering yesterday's pain" is nothing more than having a certain distinctive type of experience *now,* an experience that I surely *could* have even if there had been no such pain yesterday. The inference from my present perceptions to what I shall experience tomorrow is obviously even more shaky. Hence I am left with what might be termed a sort of solipsism of the present moment, except that there is no longer any continuing referent for the pronoun "I" nor any for the adjectives "past" and "future."

Bertrand Russell once thought he saw a way out via William James's doctrine called "neutral monism." Combining some tenets of Berkeley ("books, tables, houses are collections of ideas"), Hume ("the mind is nothing more than a bundle of perceptions"), and Wittgenstein ("the data have no owner"), he proposed in effect that there are only the data of experience; certain collections of them are minds, and other collections are physical objects. When I see a table, some of the data constituting the table are a part of my mind. When you and I see the same table, the data in my mind are not identical with those in yours, but both sets are subsets of the set or collection that is the table.

On this view, the inferential leap I make when I conclude from my present sensations the existence of an external table is not essentially different from the leap I make when I assume that the present sensation belongs to *me*, i.e., is a part of that memory- and expectation-saturated sequence of gradually changing perceptions I call "I." Perhaps there is some small philosophical gain in this, especially as a dialectical point against those phenomenlists who are skeptical of the existence of physical objects while at the same time having confidence in their own past, present, and future sense data. But, again, the skeptic will observe that, if this doctrine makes the one inference no *worse* than the other, it also makes the one no *better* than the other (and neither of them any good).

In trying to understand Russell's theory, we find it *relatively* easy to know which data are to be assigned to ourselves, for in each case one is supposed to encompass the whole sequence of one's past, present, and future experiences. But it is much more difficult to know which data are to constitute any given physical object, e.g., this table before me. In order to protect the proposition that the table would have existed even if I hadn't perceived it, as well as the more general and presumably obvious truths that the whole world existed before there were any human beings, will continue to exist long after the human race has vanished from the scene, and would have existed even if no sentient beings had ever been a part of it, Russell has to make the table consist of a vast assemblage of *possible* data: intuitively, everything that could be called "a possible appearance of the table"—an appearance to somebody, at some time, and from some point of view, and in some mode of perception.

But the notion of "a possible *X*" is so fraught with confusion as to make it practically unintelligible. Inasmuch as, even if the point of view is fixed, this table might appear to somebody, at some time, and in some circumstances to have almost any imaginable color and shape, we shall apparently have to assign to the table, from that point of view, possible sense data of all colors and shapes. But this is surely absurd. Attempts to distinguish some of the possible data as more "standard" or "legitimate" than others will founder because it is granted that what any given observer experiences under given conditions depends as much upon his own state as upon that of the objects observed. In any case, we have reached another of those philosophical junctures at which it is wise to recall Russell's aforementioned admonition about retaining a healthy sense of reality; and the plain fact is that, no matter what one may think about sense data as such, there is clearly no such thing as a possible but nonactual sense datum. Consequently, there can be no serious prospect of constructing a real external world out of such nonexistent entities.

Still another way of trying to cope with our problem was pursued by George Santayana, with the help of more than a hint from Hume. Santayana goes a long way with the skeptic, in fact all the way to the conclusion that there is absolutely no reason whatever, whether based directly on intuition or on deductive or inductive (probabilistic) inference, for believing in the existence of an external world. Consequently, according to him, we just believe in it by an act of "animal faith." He says:

> That such external things exist, that I exist myself, and live more or less prosperously in the midst of them, is a

> faith not founded on reason but precipitated in action, and in that intent, which is virtual action, involved in perception. This faith, which it would be dishonest not to confess that I share, does no violence to a sceptical analysis of experience; on the contrary, it takes advantage of that analysis to interpret this volatile experience as all animals do and must, as a set of symbols for existences that cannot enter experience, and which, since they are not elements in knowledge, no analysis of knowledge can touch—they are in another realm of being.[12]

Thus, the necessity of entertaining such belief is built into us biologically; we can't help it, even though we see that there is no reason justifying it.

But a devastating answer to this idea is given, in effect, by Berkeley and Hume. Just what is it that we are supposed to believe? Consider that table again. By animal faith I am supposed to believe in the existence of something that in some sense stands behind and is represented by what I immediately perceive. But, once again, it is acknowledged on all hands that the so-called secondary qualities, such as colors, sounds, tastes, felt heat and cold, etc., are not in the external objects themselves but are different for different observers and depend for their occurrence upon a wide variety of factors, among which the conditions of the observer's sensory apparatus and the nature of the intervening medium are at least as important as any attributes of the alleged external object. Therefore, the color I see when I look at the table and the sound I hear when I rap on it are not to be considered as attributes intrinsic to the external object itself; rather, according to the received account, they are effects of the joint action of many causes, of which the state of the table itself is only one. Thus these secondary qualities are clearly mind-dependent. Now the received account does ascribe certain other attributes, namely, the so-called primary qualities, to the external object itself. These are extension, figure, motion, solidity (perhaps), etc. The real table, while having no color, sound, or taste, is supposed to have spatial location and to consist of a buzzing galaxy of tiny particles or quark wavicles that have such attributes as mass, position, or energy and are constantly on the move.

But, as Berkeley and Hume notice, if we consider all of this a little more carefully, we see that the primary-secondary distinction, at least as regards mind-dependence, cannot be maintained. It is impossible to conceive of an object having extension and shape and absolutely no color; hence, if color is mind-dependent, so are extension and shape. The same holds for motion and spatial location. To imagine a completely colorless entity moving around is to imagine nothing; and in fact, if we try to imagine the swarm of particles that are supposed to constitute the external table that causes what we actually see, we seem forced, despite warnings from our scientific colleagues, to picture these particles as though they had, on a small scale, the colors, shapes, and other properties we are accustomed to associate with macroscopic objects and which we realize cannot exist apart from minds.

Consequently, when we are told that we must and might as well believe in the existence of a something that is somehow represented by what we perceive but that exists independently of us and hence does not number among its essential properties any of those mind-dependent qualities that we are immediately acquainted with, we really do not know how to comply. As Berkeley remarked, the real table in which we are supposed to believe is said to be visible though it has no color, to have a real shape and a real temperature though any perceived shape or temperature is admittedly mind-dependent, and so on. In short, the description we are given of the external object is essentially incoherent, and, consequently, the belief that is urged upon us is impossible. So much for the recommendation that we have "animal faith" in an external world.

It would be fair to add, I suppose, that these same considerations call into question the very meaningfulness of the thesis that nothing exists besides our perceptions. For that thesis to be meaningful, it would seem that its negation, namely, that there does exist something besides our perceptions, would have to be meaningful, too. But what sort of a "something" could that be? (I.e., what is the range of values of the existential quantifier here?) Certainly the majority of philosophers and other people who assert the existence of such "external" objects ascribe to those objects qualities similar to those they ascribe to their perceptions, and Berkeley and Hume were refuting that point of view. But is it possible to believe in a pure I-know-not-what, assigning to it only the attribute of being a nonperception? It is hard to imagine what that belief-state of mind would be like, and I do not know whether this has any real bearing on the meaningfulness of the proposition that there exists nothing in addition to our perceptions. At any rate, one thing is obvious: these considerations do nothing to solve the External World problem, and perhaps they only make it worse.

Sense Data

Still another way of attacking the problem, relatively popular in recent philosophy, is to deny that there are any such things as perceptions (or sense data, sensa, phenomena, appearances, the given, etc.). If perceptions, as this term is used in the statement of the problem, do not exist, it would seem that the main premises in the paradoxical argument are not true and hence that the pressure to accept the conclusion disappears.

Those who refuse to accept the existence of the entities in question do so on either of two mutually exclusive bases: either (1) they do not challenge the meaningfulness of the crucial terms "perception," "sense data," et al., but find that there are in fact no corresponding entities or at least that there is no good reason to "posit" such entities, or else (2) they consider the terms themselves simply devoid of meaning. The latter point of view is a special case of a more general approach that diagnoses the whole External World problem as arising from a misuse of language, and I shall discuss it in that connection later. For a prime example of the former way of treating the matter, let us consider some arguments offered by W. V. Quine against the positing of sense data.

However, we should perhaps first give some attention to what the term "sense datum," along with its various synonyms and close relatives, has been taken by epistemologists to mean.

A beginner in philosophy, untutored and inexperienced, might suppose that the way to find out what philosophers have meant by this technical term would be to look in their writings for definitions of it. One would hope that in these definitions the terminology employed would be neutral, i.e., such as to be acceptable both to those who believe in the existence of sense data and to those who do not. Then a more or less rational dispute over such existence could be carried on.

Alas, no satisfactory definition is to be found in the literature. No one has ever produced a straightforward definition that is formulated in terminology acceptable to those philosophers who refuse to accept the thesis that there are sense data, and probably no one ever will. In fact, very few of the philosophers who have used the term have even made a serious attempt to define it. Usually they have only indicated, in various ways, some of the things to which it applies, and they have set down what they consider a number of true sentences in which it occurs; and that is as far as the explanations have gone.

This is not to say, of course, that they have failed to do a satisfactory job of introducing the term or, in other words, that they have not succeeded in letting us know what they are talking about when they use it. Except in mathematics and closely related disciplines, new terminology is almost never introduced by definition. Indeed, if we understood only words that have been satisfactorily defined, ostensively or otherwise, we should understand hardly anything at all. The general term "pain," for example, which denotes any one of an indefinitely large number of particular experiences, has never been satisfactorily defined in terms of other words whose meaning we know better or knew earlier; nor, fortunately, has the whole range of its application ever been laid before us, to make possible a complete definition by ostension. Nevertheless, every speaker of English understands this word as well as he understands any other, and better than he understands most. So epistemologists are hardly to be faulted for using the term "sense datum" without first supplying adequate definitions of it.

On the other hand, it is indeed clear that the term has been used in many different ways and that its use has encouraged the posing of an abundance of nonsensical questions. But a common core in the divergent usages can easily be discerned, and prima facie there is no more reason to blame this term for the nonsensical questions in which it occurs than there would be, e.g., to blame the numeral "17" for such a question as "Is 17 purple?"

Clearly inessential to the employment of "sense datum" is the hypothesis that each datum should be associated with one and only one of the so-called senses, whether they be five in number or, as we are told has lately been discovered, twelve. Pains, anger, vague feelings of discomfort, memories, and even thought, that "dialogue of the soul with herself"—these and all other experiences have an equal claim to be counted as data. (Consequently, it would perhaps serve the interests of clarity if, in connection with the External World problem, we were to use the term "perception" or "datum of experience" instead of "sense datum.") Again, there is no implication that experience comes in layers, as it were, and that the philosopher can, with great attention and care, peer through the top layer of "preanalytic" but judgment-transformed data down to pure, raw, "postanalytic" data of sensation. On the contrary, when any special peering or looking more closely is done, the situation seems better described in terms of the occurrence of a succession of similar but nonetheless distinguishable data, some earlier and some later, than in terms of getting a more reliable view of something that remains qualitatively the same whether it is observed glancingly or intently.

The sense-datum epistemologist also has no need to subscribe to the notion that experience is a sort of granular conglomerate of data, with each datum enjoying an existence entirely independent of its surroundings. For, despite what we have been taught by Hume on this subject, there is no a priori plausibility in the thesis that, whenever there are two distinguishable data, neither of which is a part of the other, these data are also separable in the sense that either could have occurred even if the other had not. It *could* be the case, for example, that colors seen when certain kinds of sounds are heard are rather different in quality from anything that can be seen during silence; there is no a priori reason against it. Equally inessential is the view that all experience is in some way generated out of a core of elementary data, whether of sensation or of "thought." Perhaps a case can be made for such a theory, but success or failure in that enterprise would have little bearing on the matters before us.

The general characterization of sense data most frequently put forward is that they are whatever is immediately or directly perceived. This, of course, is challenged at once by those philosophers who say that they do not understand how the phrases "immediately perceived" and "directly perceived" are used here. I am inclined to say "*say* they do not understand" instead of "do not understand" because their subsequent linguistic behavior, including the appositeness of their criticisms of various assertions in which the given term occurs, suggests that they *do* understand what is intended at least as well as most of us understand most of what we hear and read. But, be that as it may, the sense-datum epistemologist's use of the words "directly perceive" is not so hopelessly inexplicable as has sometimes been made out. It involves the notion that when, for example, I am correctly said to hear Big Ben, there is in that situation at least (1) something that I do hear and that I *could* continue to hear even if Big Ben did not exist, and (2) something else, viz., Big Ben itself, that *could not* be heard if Big Ben did not exist. *By* hearing the former I hear the latter, although the former could be heard even if the latter did not exist; in this respect the perception of the former is *immediate* or *direct* relative to that of the latter. If the perception of something X is such that there is nothing else the perception of which is immediate relative to that perception of X, then that perception of X may be called immediate or direct *simpliciter.*[13]

General characterizations of the data are usually supplemented by express mention of specific classes of cases. For instance, it is said that tastes, colors, sounds, smells, felt hardnesses and roughnesses, pains, dreams, thoughts, and so on are data. To fend off certain (usually philosophically motivated) misunderstandings, one adds immediately such caveats as that the term "sounds" here refers to what psychologists have sometimes called "heard sounds" and not to vibrations in the air or events in the nervous system. Scientists tell us that, although what is directly heard is normally the *effect* of vibrations in the air, it can be caused in other ways, too; in any case, it is not to be identified with those vibrations. Similar considerations apply if an attempt is made to identify heard sounds with neural excitations, although in this case the matter is somewhat more complex because heard sounds happen to correlate more uniformly with states of neural excitation than they do with the occurrence of pressure waves in the air.[14]

If the use of "sense datum" or "datum of experience" is still not sufficiently clear, the epistemologist will list other terms having approximately the same denotation. To anyone who feels the need of a definition, of course, these other terms are likely to seem even more vague and problematic than the ones being explicated. The expression "sense datum" itself is of relatively recent origin; it was probably introduced in the period 1880–90 and was given philosophical currency by Bertrand Russell and G. E. Moore around 1910. But philosophers have always had nomenclature, more or less technical, for essentially the same purpose. In Plato and Aristotle we find the word *phainomena;* the Stoic term was *phantasiai* (usually translated as "presentations"); Berkeley and the other British Empiricists use "ideas," "ideas in the mind," or "impressions"; Kant and his tradition have *Vorstellungen;* other words are "sensa," "sensibilia," "percepts," and "appearances"; and, for the totality, there are "the given," "the sensible manifold," or "the manifold of experience."

As has often been pointed out, everyone who uses these expressions recognizes that none of them is quite right. To call the data "appearances" may suggest that every datum is an appearance of something else; the example of pains is sufficient to refute this, and it seems that even such data as are appearances, in the strict sense of that term, are only contingently so. Again, to some people "the given" suggests a giver, but surely the sense-datum terminology does not commit its adherents to any such quasi-theological view. And the term "sense datum" itself may seem to connote that the stream of experience is made up of a number of separable patches, each of which is one datum, or that it is all derived from sense. But, as we noticed earlier, no such hypotheses are required. The crucial point here would seem to be that, in order for us to understand discourse that contains the term "sense datum" and is otherwise acceptable, it suffices that we know what is being talked about, i.e., denoted; in epistemological discussions the (Fregean) senses, if any, of the various terms used to denote the data are usually irrelevant.

Finally, let us note one other way in which the suspect terminology is commonly introduced, This involves first distinguishing two senses of such verbs as "to hear" and "to see" and is in effect an elaboration of the "directly perceive" approach. Suppose that Smith and Jones are looking at the Campanile from different points of view; the light is good, and neither of them has any difficulty seeing it. Then consider the assertion:

Smith and Jones see the same thing.

Is it true or is it false? Well, on the one hand, of course it is true, for *ex hypothesi* Smith and Jones both see the Campanile. On the other hand, since what anyone sees in a given situation depends upon his perspective, the lighting, and the whole structure and state of his nervous system, it is equally obvious that what Smith sees under these circumstances is not even "congruent," let alone literally identical, with what is seen by Jones. Now, no sentence can be both true and false when taken in the same sense; consequently, we are led to the conclusion that our assertion has more than one sense. It is natural to single out the verb "see" as the culprit and to say that there are two (or at least two) senses of this word.[15] In one sense, what one sees is ordinarily all or part of a material object; in this sense it is possible and indeed quite usual for a number of persons to see exactly the same thing.[16] In another sense, what each individual sees is "private" to him insofar as its nature and very existence always depend upon the peculiarities of his own constitution. What is seen, in *this* sense, is a sense datum.

The same distinctions apply, *mutatis mutandis,* to verbs for hearing and the other forms of perception. In one sense of "hear," we say that we hear bells, trains, fire engines, etc.; in another, that we hear only *sounds*. Note that it does not seem difficult to give at least a rough indication of how these two senses of "hear" are related, which would hardly be possible if we did not have some understanding of the distinction. Ordinarily, what counts as hearing a fire engine, for example, is hearing a certain sound that is made by a fire engine, though in a further sense of "hear" it might be required in addition that the sound be *taken* as coming from a fire engine.

In any case, it seems incontestable that if I honestly report, on the basis of the familiar auditory experience, that I hear a fire engine, and if later, by adducing other evidence, you are able to convince me that it was a police car, my yielding on this does not require revising my view of the nature of what I heard (in at least one sense of "hear"). That view may remain constant while I switch my opinion about the causes. Evén if at length it were established that no fire engine, police car, ambulance, or siren or any other such "external" object was within hearing distance at the time, the conclusion would clearly not be justified that I heard nothing or that I do not know what I heard.

The foregoing, none of which will be news to the journeyman philosopher, should give some idea of what epistemologists are talking about when they use the terms "sense datum" or "datum of experience." If there is a problem about what constitutes *one* datum, it can be resolved simply as follows: every part of a datum is a datum, and every fusion of data is again a datum.

With this background, let us now examine what Quine has to say about the matter. For him, if I understand him correctly, the question whether sense data exist runs over into, or is in effect replaced by, the question whether "any sufficient purpose is served by positing" such objects, where to posit a wide class of objects is to make a decision to use language in a certain way. In the present case his verdict is negative: "no sufficient purpose is served by positing subjective sensory events." To support this, he sketches three arguments.

> (a) It would be argued that we cannot hope to make such objects suffice to the exclusion of physical objects. This point . . . seems pretty widely acknowledged nowadays. (b) It would be argued . . . that we do not need them in addition to physical objects, as means e.g. of reporting illusions and uncertainties. Thus one might claim that such purposes are adequately met by a propositional-attitude construction in which "seems that" or the like is made to govern a subsidiary sentence about physical objects . . . (c) It would be argued that we also do not need sensory objects to account for our knowledge or discourse of physical objects themselves. The claim here would be that the relevance of sensory stimulation to sentences about physical objects can as well (and better) be explored and explained in terms directly of the conditioning of such sentences or their parts to physical irritations of the subject's surfaces. Intervening neural activity goes on, but the claim is that nothing is clarified, nothing but excess baggage is added, by positing intermediary subjective objects of apprehension anterior to the physical objects overtly alleged in the spoken sentences themselves.[17]

The first of these arguments ("we cannot hope to make such objects suffice to the exclusion of physical objects") is presumably directed against what might be called the linguistic form of phenomenalism, namely, the thesis that any sentence about physical objects is translatable into a sentence referring exclusively to the data of sense. Now, it is indeed true that from the start this thesis has had rough going. Opponents have been able to point out that not a single example of such translation has ever been given; they have argued that the project is impossible because the sense-data sentence would have to be infinitely long and that at best it could express only conditions confirming, rather than completely verifying, the physical-object sentence; and now they bring forward the clincher, that in any case the only way we can refer to sense data is by using sentences that also contain terms referring to physical objects.

At one level, objections like these are always answerable, it seems to me, if only we bear in mind that the intuitive idea behind the claim that sentences about physical objects should be translatable into sentences about data is roughly this: every meaningful synthetic sentence must be verifiable or at least confirmable in the given, so the cognitive content of a meaningful sentence should be expressible by the totality of sentences describing just those experiences that would tend to confirm it. Thus, difficulties about sentences that are infinitely long may be sidestepped by considering sets of sentences instead, and one may wish to interpret "translatable" as referring to a relation of maximum confirmation rather than a relation of strict synonymy or even of logical equivalence. In response to "the clincher," the thesis could be reworded to get rid of the requirement that the sentences about sense data should contain no physical-object terms. After all, in describing an afterimage, one might say that a portion of it is the color of an orange; such a description, even though it contains an (oblique) occurrence of a physical-object term, would nonetheless be a description of a sense datum.

But there is something fundamentally unsatisfactory about playing this game, as though its outcome would decide the question whether sense data exist. The root of the matter, I think, is that it is for the most part completely unintuitive to equate questions of existence with questions of what way it is advantageous to talk. Even in mathematics, where such an outlook is perhaps most often accepted, carryover from habits of nonmathematical discourse makes many persons wary of regarding so-called external questions about the existence of numbers or sets, for example, as disguised questions about the utility of adopting certain conventions of language. And when we come to such down-to-earth items as sounds, colors, tastes, pains, etc., instead of abstract entities like numbers, points, lines, and sets, it is difficult not to feel that to make *their* existence depend in any way upon utility or simplicity of theory is to put the cart before the horse. It is hard to conceive of a rational philosophy of language that does not accept the idea that language is only part of the world, that there is, in addition, some sort of extralinguistic reality, the existence and nature of which does not depend upon or in any essential way reflect the vagaries of our linguistic behavior. It must be obvious that, even if all language and linguistic behavior were suddenly obliterated, it would make precious little difference to what *exists* in the extralinguistic world, despite a maximal change in what could be said and what was useful to say.

So, the short answer to the claim that not every sentence about physical objects is translatable into a sentence referring exclusively to the data of sense is that this claim, even if true, is irrelevant to the question whether the data exist.

The same kinds of consideration weigh against Quine's second point, that we do not need sense data in addition to material objects as means of reporting illusions and uncertainties. He suggests that we could use the phrase "it seems that . . . ," followed by a sentence plainly referring to material objects, to describe the same situations that some philosophers have thought were best described by sentences referring overtly to sense data. Gilbert Ryle makes a similar proposal and adds, as further possibilities, the phrases "it looks as if . . . ," "it has the appearance of . . . ," "I might be seeing . . . ."[18] Thus, a squinter, or a person doing the ancient eyeball-pressing epistemological experiment, might say, "It looks as if there were two candles on the table" and insist that this describes the perceptual situation as well as, or better than, any statement to the effect that he does see two bright somethings.

Now, despite its essential irrelevance to the issue before

us, i.e., to the question whether sense data exist, this claim is interesting in its own right. As Socrates says, let us give the pot a couple of raps to see if it is sound; let us digress long enough to consider some particular cases and look for translations along the lines suggested.

There are certain types of situations—namely, those in which one wishes to state a similarity between a sense datum that is normally caused and one that is not—that seem very difficult to handle in the way proposed. Suppose, for example, that I am bothered by a ringing in the ear and that this ringing sound has a definite pitch. I go over to the piano and, after a little experimentation, establish that the pitch of my ringing sound is approximately that of the sound produced by striking a certain key—which happens to be E above middle C. Referring to sense data, I might say that there are two sense data here, the sound of the piano, as heard by me, and the ringing sound that is presumably not caused by any external object, and, further, that these two sounds have the same pitch. How shall I describe the same phenomenon by means of a sentence of the approved type? I cannot just say

> It seems that I hear a bell and a piano that
> are sounding at the same pitch,

for of course that leaves out the fact that I *do* hear the piano sound. I could try

> I hear a piano sounding E, and it seems that
> I hear a bell sounding E,

but that won't work, because it involves a definite specification of the pitch, whereas I want only to report the sameness. Neither

> The pitch of the piano sound that I do hear
> is the same as the pitch of the bell sound I
> seem to hear

nor

> The piano that I hear is sounding-at-the-same-pitch-as the bell that I seem to hear

will do, for in these cases we do not have "it seems that" governing a sentence. Another possibility would be (borrowing some notation from logic)

> ($\exists x$) (I hear a piano sound of pitch x and it seems that I hear a bell sound of pitch x).

But this sort of quantification, as Quine himself has very convincingly shown, will lead to paradox because of the referential opacity of contexts generated by expressions like "it seems that."

Thus it is by no means clear that the phenomena can always be satisfactorily described by a compound of material-object sentences and sentences that result from prefixing expressions like "it seems that" to material-object sentences. Since illusions and veridical experiences may contain common (or at least similar) elements, it seems necessary that, in the descriptions of illusions, certain constituent expressions should occur in contexts accessible to quantification.

Quine's third point is that we do not need sensory objects to account for our knowledge or discourse about physical objects. I don't know whether we do or not. But, twanging the same string once more: from "We do not need *X* to account for *Y*" it is a long way to "*X* does not exist."

So much for the question whether sense data exist. But now, to quote Socrates once more, we proceed to *to kephalaion*, "the crown" of this part of our deliberations: *The existence or nonexistence of sense data, perceptions, ideas—call them what you will—is really irrelevant to the External World problem anyway*. For we can state the problem without committing ourselves on that issue one way or the other.

With respect to perceptual judgments, it is usual to distinguish between the way things are and the way they seem to be. (Here the word "thing" is used syncategorematically, of course, and not as a name for a special class of entities.) The way things are is supposed to be independent of the observer; at least, this is supposed to be the case when we are perceiving the macroscopic objects with which most of our perceptual judgments are concerned. But the way things seem to be, e.g., to me, is supposed to depend upon me as well as upon what I observe. Further, it is recognized that things could seem to me to be the way they do now even if they weren't the way they are; this is at least abstractly, logically possible. But clearly, in the relevant cases, our perceptual judgments about how things are are ultimately based on how they seem to us; any checking or confirming of initial impressions consists merely in a further determination of how things seem. Thus, even if things were not at all the way they are, they could seem to be the way they do seem, and, if they did so seem, we would have the same basis for our perceptual judgments that we do now, even though many of those judgments would be completely mistaken. Consequently, in perceptual judgments we have no knowledge of how things are but only, at most, knowledge of how they seem to be; and hence in these cases we have no knowledge of anything that is supposed to exist independently of ourselves.

Or, suppose that Ryle and Quine are right in suggesting that what seems to be the case can adequately be described by sentences consisting of one of the phrases "it seems that," "it looks as if," etc., followed by a sentence plainly referring to material objects only. Then the External World problem consists in this: (1) no nontrivial material-object sentence follows from any collection, however large, of sentences introduced by these phrases; (2) ultimately the only evidence we can have for a knowledge-claim about the perceptual attributes of material objects (e.g., their color, shape, solidity, etc.) is expressible by sentences of the "it seems that" variety.

So, evidently, the External World problem does not hinge on how one arranges one's epistemological ontology. All that is required to appreciate the conundrum is a realization that we can in every case make the same kinds of mistakes we sometimes make in judging how things are from how they seem to be. Philosophers have hoped that somehow logic would show that it is impossible to make more than a certain number of mistakes of this type without getting something else right, but, alas, no such cheering argument has come forth.

SENSE AND NONSENSE

After more than two millennia of utterly unsuccessful philosophical efforts to solve the problem before us or to refute the skepticism that gives rise to it, philosophers were moved inevitably to ask themselves whether the questions at issue even made sense. Recent philosophy, at least in England and America, has been dominated by this aspect. The preoccupation with language, so annoying to those many observers who complain that philosophers nowadays no longer tackle the "big questions," is no doubt largely motivated by the continual failure to make any progress when considering such questions head-on.

The approach to philosophical problems through the study of language has taken two forms. On the one hand, the so-called Logical Positivists put forward and defended a new criterion of meaning—the verifiability criterion—according to which it turned out that our central question, "How can I have knowledge of anything other than my own present perceptions?", was found to be devoid of cognitive content. They also raised questions about the admissibility of certain crucial terms occurring in the statements of the problem. In line with their verifiability criterion, they found these terms lacking in empirical content, in the sense that usually the corresponding sentences "There are *X*s" for such a term *X* would be absolutely unverifiable. Another approach is that of the so-called Ordinary Language group, led by J. L. Austin. He proposed to "dismantle the problem before it could get off the ground"[19] by showing that in its typical formulations there is an abuse of language; that is, either pseudo-technical terms (e.g., "sense data," "sensibilia," "percepts") are introduced in an unsatisfactory way, or ordinary words (e.g., "appearances," "experience," "sensations") are used, without explanation, in extraordinary or stretched senses. I shall consider these two approaches in order.

The Verifiability Criterion of Meaning

The proponents of the verifiability criterion were the members of the Vienna Circle, including, most notably, Moritz Schlick and Rudolf Carnap. Seeking a satisfactory basis for distinguishing the relatively clear and intelligible assertions of science and common sense, on the one hand, from the obscure and confusing propositions of metaphysics, on the other, they thought they had found such a basis in a criterion of meaning: a declarative sentence is cognitively meaningful if and only if it is verifiable in the given. "To verify," in this connection, means "to discover the truth-value of," not "to determine to be true." (Necessary truths and their negations are to be considered limiting cases of sentences verifiable in the given.)

The difference between "verifiable" and "verified" was emphasized by Schlick and the other advocates of the theory. For a sentence to be meaningful, they said, there must be some way of verifying it; i.e., it must in principle be capable of verification, but there is no need that its truth-value be actually known. The only kinds of grammatically correct sentences that are deemed "devoid of cognitive content" are those that are such that by no conceivable experience could it ever be determined whether what they assert is or is not the case.

For a (rather artificial) example, consider the following hypothesis. Whenever you and I look at the same object, the color that I see is always located a little further along the spectrum from the one you see. If the object looks red to you, it looks orangish-red to me, and, if it looks orangish-red to you, it looks orange to me, and so on. My range of color perception is slightly extended at one end of the spectrum, and yours at the other, so that, whenever two objects are distinguishable in color for either of us, they are also distinguishable for the other. However, since we have both learned the use of color words by "ostensive definitions," in which colored objects were presented and appropriately labeled, our differences in perception are exactly offset by our linguistic habits. Thus, when you look at a given object and call it "red," I apply the same word, for I have learned to apply that word when I see a color to which, if you could see it, you would apply the term "orangish-red."

It seems that no test will reveal whether in fact we are in the circumstances just described. We would agree in our answers to all ordinary questions of the form "What color is *X*?" We would agree when asked, on any given occasion, how many colors we see. We would agree when asked whether *X* is darker than *Y*, whether *X* is more like *Y* than it is like *Z*, and so forth. Neurological investigations will not help, either, for of course no two nervous systems are going to be in exactly the same condition at any particular time anyway.

Thus it appears that the hypothesis is completely unverifiable. Consequently, the verifiability criterion would rule it out as being cognitively meaningless. To be sure, it may have a certain amount of "emotive" content, perhaps making us feel that in some sense we are more alone in the world than we had heretofore realized, but its cognitive content is nil. It goes out as nonsense. "Well," the reader will say, "small loss."

If the positivists are right, however, our inconsequential

little theory about color perception will be accompanied to the scrap heap of nonsense by a formidable array of what are sometimes considered to be the most sublime creations of the human mind: metaphysics and theology (including the latter-day theologies of Marxism and Freudian psychology), most of epistemology, political theory and ethics, and even certain very general hypotheses from the hard and soft sciences. In particular, all the traditional problems of philosophy will be dismissed as having no solutions, the reason being that the questions themselves are devoid of sense.

Needless to say, this doctrine caused a considerable stir. To the delight of graduate students and other tough-minded types, the positivistic fox's entry into the philosophical henhouse produced a great flapping of wings and raising of dust as the metaphysicians and epistemologists all flew off their perches together. Nor was calm reintroduced by the assurance that there is such a thing as "emotive content," which the cognitively empty theories might nevertheless be conceded to have. So, for several decades, the positivists were considered by many philosophers to be Satan's own company, and even nowadays one occasionally finds them castigated in the literature.

By this time, however, the dust has settled, and we can see that somehow the fox has failed to finish off a single one of his intended victims. A number of serious defects in the verifiability criterion have appeared, most of them discovered, incidentally, not by its opponents but by its advocates.

One obvious difficulty concerns the expression "the given." All of the positivists were of an empiricist bent, taking verification to be something that involves sensory experience; but they differed as to whether "the given" consists of the sense data themselves, or the physical states presumably causing the data, or neither of these. To agree to either of the first two possibilities would seem to involve acceptance of one of the very pseudo-distinctions the criterion was intended to extirpate. For Schlick, however, who chooses the third possibility, the verification of a statement consisted ultimately in a comparison of that statement with "the facts"; if a corresponding fact exists, the statement is true; if not, it is false.[20] The simplest statements (examples: "Here yellow borders on blue," "Here, now, pink," "Here two black points coincide") are said always to involve demonstratives and to be understandable only with the help of gestures, with which "one must somehow point to reality." Clearly, this position is no more free of metaphysics than are its competitors; to say that reality consists of facts is no more and no less intelligible than to say that it consists of physical objects or of sense data.

In order to avoid using expressions like "the given," "sense data," "physical objects," "facts," etc., attempts were made to formulate the criterion in terms of the concept "observation sentences" (sometimes called "protocol sentences"). An observation sentence is said to be a sentence that asserts of one or more specifically named physical objects that they have, or they lack, some specified observable characteristic. Examples given by Carl Hempel are "The Eiffel Tower is taller than the buildings in its vicinity," "The pointer of this instrument does not cover the point marked '3' on the scale," and even "The largest dinosaur on exhibit in New York's Museum of Natural History had a blue tongue."[21] Other authors gave quite different kinds of examples, and it was only to be expected that the problems with "the given" would carry over to the concept of protocol or observation sentences. At any rate, the criterion could now be formulated as follows: A declarative sentence has (cognitive) meaning if and only if it either is analytic (i.e., is a necessary truth or a negation of such) or follows logically from some consistent set of observation sentences.[22]

For many reasons this formulation proved unacceptable. Taken literally, it rules out all sentences of universal form (for there is no assurance that every object has a name), and hence there will be cases in which it rules out a given sentence (e.g., "Everything is blue") while accepting its negation ("Something is not blue"). Also, as understood by its proponents, it seems to involve a vicious circle: cognitive meaningfulness is defined in terms of logical consequence, a relation that in turn is defined only for meaningful sentences; hence, one cannot determine whether a given sentence *S* follows from some observation sentences unless one has already determined whether *S* is meaningful.

Perhaps one could attempt to get around the second of these difficulties by giving a syntactical definition of logical consequence, allowing the relation to hold among nonsensical statements as well as among those with congitive content. But then we would have unfortunate cases like "Either the Absolute is perfect or something is blue," which would follow from the observation sentence "This book is blue."

Carnap and some others concluded that the difficulties with the verifiability criterion were essentially due to the mistake of requiring complete verifiability rather than mere testability. For a sentence to have cognitive content, it should be sufficient, they thought, that the sentence be somehow confirmable in experience; there should, at least, be possible observations that would raise or lower its probability. In other words, any nonanalytic sentence that is so remote from experience that the degree of probability we attach to it will not be affected no matter what is observed is cognitively meaningless.

This idea is intuitively very attractive, but the task of expressing it with adequate precision has proved unexpectedly difficult. In the first edition of his *Language, Truth and Logic,* A. J. Ayer defined a sentence *S* as confirmable if and only if there is an observation sentence *O* and a set of auxiliary hypotheses *H* which are such that *O* follows from *S* together with *H* but not from *H* alone.[23] But this had the unwelcome consequence of ascribing confirmability to almost all sentences, for, letting *O* be any observation sentence and *S* be any sentence that does not follow from the negation of *O*, *O* will follow from *S* together with the auxiliary hypothesis "If *S*, then *O*" but not from the auxiliary hypothesis alone. To remedy this sort of defect, Ayer in his second edition amended the definition in such a way as to require that the auxiliary hypotheses be themselves independently established as confirmable. But then Alonzo Church showed that, on the amended definition, if there are any three logically independent observation sentences O_1, O_2, O_3, then, for any sentence *S*, either *S* or its negation is confirmable. For, he writes,

> Let $\bar{O}_1$ and $\bar{S}$ be the negations of O_1 and *S* respectively. Then (under Ayer's definition) $\bar{O}_1 O_2 \vee O_3 \bar{S}$ is directly verifiable, because with O_1 it entails O_3. Moreover *S* and $\bar{O}_1 O_2 \vee O_3 \bar{S}$ together entail O_2. Therefore (under Ayer's definition) *S* is indirectly verifiable—unless it happens that $\bar{O}_1 O_2 \vee O_3 \bar{S}$ alone entails O_2, in which case $\bar{S}$ and O_3 together entail O_2, so that $\bar{S}$ is directly verifiable.

Because of such discouraging difficulties as these, more recent attempts to formulate an empiricist criterion of meaning have in effect defined a meaningful sentence as one that is built up by acceptable means of syntactical combination (e.g., negation, disjunction, conjunction, conditionalization, universal and existential quantification, etc.) from an initial stock of names, variables, and observation predicates.[25] We see at once, however, that the External World problem, as well as most of the other traditional problems of philosophy, will be left unscathed by this approach. For although they certainly do present difficulties of verification or even confirmation, they are stated without violation of the rules of syntax and without the use of clearly nonempirical terminology.

Let us next consider some of the doubts that have been

raised about the meaning or use of various crucial terms that occur in typical formulations of our problem.

"What would it be like to find that . . . ?"

In a very influential article first published more than forty years ago, G. A. Paul sets out to consider the question whether sense data exist.[26] But he says that he is unable to come to any decision about this because he cannot find out what the problem is. The difficulty, according to him, is to understand what anyone is saying who says that there *are* such things as sense data. It is not solely due, he thinks,

> to the fact that a word is being introduced which has not been used before, for there are many cases in which this is done where there is no such difficulty. For example, the physiologists who wished to introduce the word "fovea" to describe a certain peculiarity of the structure of the eye can have encountered no such difficulty. They could say that they were using "fovea" as a name for the slight depression in the retina diametrically opposite to the pupil, and by dissecting eyes could point to instances of this depression.[27]

The crucial difference between the terms "fovea" and "sense datum," in Paul's opinion, is that in the former case we can decide by experiment whether foveae exist, for "we have some idea of what it will be like to find such a depression and of what it will be like to be unable to find such a depression or to find that there is no such depression"; whereas, in the case of sense data, we have no idea what it would be like to find that there were none.

There are several difficulties with this line of argument. First, the implied criterion for the meaningfulness of a general term is unsatisfactory. There are many different reasons, some of which have little to do with meaning, why one might not know "what it would be like to find that such-and-such." This becomes especially clear when we have the kind of partial self-reference exhibited in the following examples: What would it be like to find that one was located at the center of the sun? What would it be like to find that, contrary to Newton, bodies repel one another with a force inversely proportional to the square of the distance between them? What would it be like to find that the human race was entirely extinct? What would it be like to find that one was unconscious, or dead, or that one had never existed? So we need not be dismayed by the evident difficulty involved in answering the question, "What would it be like to find that there were no sense data?"

But in the second place, if the question is slightly differently formulated as "What would it be like if there were no data?" (not "What would it be like to *find* that there were no data"), it has for each of us, I suppose, a fairly obvious answer: that would be like unconsciousness, dreamless sleep, or death. Whoever has no feelings, sees nothing, hears nothing, tastes nothing, thinks nothing, etc., is, one would be inclined to say, either unconscious or dead.

Paul attaches considerable significance to another point. "The word 'fovea,'" he says, "was introduced as a name for a physical object, and we know how to use it in new cases because we know in general how words for physical objects are used in English . . . The new word is brought into use as a member of a class of words whose use in certain contexts is already given."[28] This, presumably, is supposed to contrast it with "sense datum," which is not introduced as a name for a kind of physical object.

Now sense-data epistemologists, from Berkeley onward, have always acknowledged that ordinary language seems best fitted for discourse about physical objects and that many assertions and questions that are significant when applied to these objects are odd or unintelligible when we attempt to refer them to data. Thus the question "Are sense data located inside the brain?" is of dubious status as regards meaning, and the question "What does the far side of a visual sense datum look like?" is pretty obviously nonsense. If one is asked whether sense data can appear to be other than they really are, one feels again that something is wrong with the question. Data most typically *are* appearances, and it is not clear what can be meant by asking of an appearance whether it can appear to be other than it is. But the point of all this for the sense-datum epistemologist is quite different from the point it has for Paul. For the former the interesting feature is that we *can* recognize a bogus question about sense data when we see one, and that, he thinks, is an indication that in large measure we do know what we are talking about when we use the term.

In passing, it may also be observed that Paul's statement about how the term "sense datum" has been introduced is factually incorrect. Although "sense datum" is not brought into use as a word standing for physical objects (neither, strictly, is "fovea"), it *is* "brought in as a member of a class of words whose use in certain contexts is already given." Other members of the class are the words "pain," "sound," "taste," and "feeling." This is not to say that "sense datum" can be used in any and all contexts in which these other terms may be used; but no such complete interchangeability is found in the case of terms for physical objects, either.

How To Talk

In a variant on Paul's approach, Professors Ryle and Austin and many others have argued that the whole sense-datum–material-object distinction rests on the misuse of certain words. Ryle traces the difficulty to what he calls "the logical howler . . . of assimilating the concept of sensation to the concept of observation"; according to him, when we describe all sensation as the observing of certain objects, namely, sense data, we are misusing the word "observe."[29] Austin does not like the sense-datum theorist's use of the word "given," "for this suggests (a) that something is here 'given' us by somebody; (b) that sensa are called 'given' in contrast with something which is rather 'made' or 'taken,' namely, my thoughts." Also, he denies not only that there are in fact the two senses of "see" distinguished by the sense-datum theorist but also that the phrases "directly perceive" and "immediately perceive" are used by epistemologists in their ordinary senses. When "immediately perceive" is explained with the help of the expression "visual field," he complains that no explanation is given of *that.*[30]

Instead of considering these objections in detail, I shall outline a general response to all who argue that there is something improper, illegitimate, or defective about the way in which the term "sense datum" is introduced by philosophers. My remarks will apply equally to "perceptions" and all the other members of the "call-them-what-you-will" vocabulary.

The gist of what I have to say is that the manner in which "sense datum" has been brought into use is not essentially different from what we find in a large number of perfectly ordinary cases and that much of the criticism is inspired by the mistaken idea that whatever unclarity may attend the words by means of which the use of a new expression is explained must necessarily attach to the new expression itself. This mistaken idea is perhaps derived from the tendency to take the giving of definitions as the only way, or the ideal way, in which a new expression can properly be introduced or an old term sharpened for technical use.

It must be granted that, when we speak of "introducing a *new* expression into the language" (where "introduction" refers to some sort of act specifically designed to convey a relatively large amount of semantic and syntactic information about the given expression), we are already moving away from fact and into the realm of idealization.

In the kinds of cases under consideration here, it seldom if ever happens that a term is introduced absolutely de novo. Ordinarily we gradually learn to use a given linguistic expression by being present when it is used by others; even on those infrequent occasions when we are favored with an explicit definition or a group of axioms or some other such directly relevant material, we usually have had a significant amount of advance acquaintance with the term in question. This point must be kept in mind as a general qualification of the account that follows.

Let us recall the Fregean distinction between the sense and the denotation of linguistic expressions,[31] and with reference to that let us note that when a new expression is to be brought into use, or an old one further explained, there are, basically and roughly, two ways in which this may be accomplished: either (1) by characterizing the sense of the given expression or (2) by indicating its denotation without attempting to convey the sense. Observe that, although the sense of an expression determines the denotation (if any), yet, to give the sense is not thereby to give the denotation; for whether a certain object is included in the denotation corresponding to a given sense is often a contingent matter or, even if not contingent, a matter that is not easy to settle.

It is true, as will be seen in the examples to be discussed below, that actual cases seem to combine these two elements in varying degrees; that is to say, when semantic information is given, some of what is said or done is put forward (and taken) as partially characterizing the sense, and some of it seems to serve only the function of pointing out (or otherwise identifying) the denotation.

The sense of an expression may be given completely by means of a definition in terms of other expressions whose senses are already understood, or it may be given partially by laying down as axioms or so-called meaning-postulates certain sentences in which the expression under consideration occurs. A way of testing whether, in a given case, there has been a characterization of the sense (and not merely an indication of the denotation) is to note whether the definition or axioms are taken as generating a corresponding set of "new" (nonformal) necessary truths. If, for example, the word "circle" is defined in a mathematical context as "a closed plane curve such that all of its points are equidistant from a single point," we take this phrase as giving, for that context at least, the sense of the word "circle." If someone were to raise the question: "Could there be a circle that was not a closed plane curve?" the answer would seem to be "Of course not, unless the term 'circle' is used in a somewhat different (perhaps metaphorical, or more general) sense." Thus the definition is taken in such a way as to generate a whole new family of nonformal necessary truths, of which "Every circle is a closed plane curve" would be one member.

Note that the necessity here is due to the way in which the definition is taken and not to the fact that the subject matter is mathematical. Thus, compare the dictionary definition of "brother": "A male being related to others (male or female) as the child of the same parent or parents." On this definition, it does not just *happen* that all brothers are male; it is *impossible* for things to be otherwise. Another example would be the definition of "flotilla" as "a small fleet or a fleet of small vessels." It is clear that the sentence "There is a flotilla that is neither a small fleet nor a fleet of small vessels" expresses an impossibility as long as the word "flotilla" is used in accord with this definition.

For contrast, consider Webster's definition of "green" as "a color the hue of which is somewhat less yellow than that of growing grass or of the emerald." Surely we do not take this definition as implying that "grass is yellowish green" and "emeralds are yellowish green" are necessary truths. The lexicographer is telling us, rather, that green is the color that growing grass and emeralds happen in fact to have; presumably things could have been otherwise. Similarly, when the dictionary explains "pain" as "a feeling proceeding from a derangement of functions, disease, or bodily injury," it can hardly be interpreted as denying that "pains are caused by bodily injury" is a contingent truth. The reference to bodily injury, like the reference to grass and emeralds, helps us identify the denotation of the word defined, but it tells us little if anything about the sense.

Just as a properly constructed "ordinary" definition is, under certain not easily specified circumstances, a paradigm vehicle for conveying semantic information about the sense of the defined expression, so also what are called "ostensive definitions" would, I suppose, be the paradigmatic devices for indicating denotation without any explicit commitment in regard to sense. Natural examples of ostensive definitions are hard to find, mainly because the whole idea is largely a philosophers' myth with no simple counterpart in the real world. Nevertheless, it is clear that actual cases do occasionally exhibit some of the features under consideration here.

Suppose, for example, that on your first trip along the Grand Canal someone, for your benefit, points at a certain building on the left and says, "Ca' d'Oro." Or, he might point at it and say "That is the Ca' d'Oro." Or, he might omit the pointing and just say, "On the left is the Ca' d'Oro." In each of these cases, I think, it would not be unreasonable to describe him as drawing your attention to the building that is the denotation of the term "Ca' d'Oro" and as making you understand that this building is the denotation of that term. Whether he does it by giving an arm gesture while uttering the term in question, or by giving an arm gesture while uttering a whole sentence, or just by talking seems inessential. In none of these three cases, including the last one, does he tell you anything about the sense (if any) of the name "Ca' d'Oro." Your stock of necessary truths containing this term is no greater after the successful completion of the performance than it was before; in particular, even if what was said was "On the left is the Ca' d'Oro," there will be no necessary truth to the effect that the Ca' d'Oro was on your left at a certain moment of time. The sentence in question does give important semantic information about the name "Ca' d'Oro," as well as expressing a matter of fact concerning the relative positions of the speaker and the building, but it would not be taken as characterizing the sense.

Clearly inessential in this example, I think, is the fact that at the time the words were uttered the denoted object was within pointing range. Nothing important would have been changed if, before the palace came into view, the guide had said, "Around the next bend, as we approach the Rialto Bridge, you will see on your left a strikingly beautiful palace, the Ca' D'Oro." And, indeed, only the pleasure but not the philosophy is affected if, instead of enjoying on-the-spot instruction about the wonders of Venice, you are sitting in your study at home, reading a guidebook. There you might find: "Ca' d'Oro: the most elegant palace in Venice"; but again the only semantic information about "Ca' d'Oro" imparted by these words concerns the denotation, not the sense. There is not the slightest suggestion that the Ca' d'Oro could not have been designed other than it was or that it would have been absolutely impossible for anyone to have built a Venetian palace that was more elegant than it.

Not only may the object of one of these "deictic" performances be out of actual pointing range, it need not even be theoretically accessible. Consider, for example, the name "Aristotle" as discussed by Frege in a famous footnote to "On Sense and Reference."[32] Even if the beginning student of the history of philosophy is told that "Aristotle was a Greek philosopher who was born in Stagira and was the teacher of Alexander the Great," he will never dream of taking "Aristotle was born in Stagira" as a necessary truth. He learns only that the denotation of the name "Aristotle" was a man who happened in fact to be a Greek philosopher born in Stagira, etc.; the denotation is indicated, but there is no information given as to the sense.

These distinctions apply not only to names of individuals but also to general terms. We have already considered the word "green." One endeavors to give a young child useful semantic information about this word by pointing out various green objects. But that does not amount to specifying its sense. However many green things are used in the performance, there would be no contradiction whatever in saying that any or all of them might not have been green. And there is no reason why such a deictic performance should not be accomplished, as indeed it is by Webster, by the use of language instead of by physical pointing.

Often, therefore, though by no means always, when a new term is introduced or the use of an old one is further explained, what is said serves only to indicate the denotation. All that one expects then is that the discourse employed should actually succeed in its deictic or quasi-deictic function; there is no necessity that it should itself have a perfectly clear sense. When, on the other hand, the goal is to give the sense of an expression, success will ordinarily depend on the extent to which the sense of the terminology utilized in the explanation is itself clear to the reader or listener. For to give the sense of an expression *is* to set forth certain analytic relationships of that term to other expressions of the language, and this is usually done by making clear how the given term is related to other expressions whose relationships to the rest of the language (i.e., whose senses) have been clearly established.

In the simplest cases of this type, a new term is introduced by informing the reader in effect that it is synonymous (i.e., interchangeable, either generally or with restrictions) with some other expression the synonymies of which are already (or perhaps are soon to be) specified. But when the aim is only to help the reader identify the denotation of the given term, it is not of primary importance that the terminology utilized be clear in sense, any more than it is crucially important, when someone is pointing out an object of interest, that his arm and finger be exactly straight or that they be exactly in line with the object in question. The crux is rather that the gesture and the talk should in fact succeed in drawing attention to what is denoted.

It is obvious that what philosophers say when introducing the term "sense datum" and its relatives should be taken in this deictic way. They say, for example, that a sense datum is what is immediately perceived or that it is what is given in experience, but this is not to be taken as information that the sense of the term "sense datum" is the same as that of the words "what is immediately perceived" or that of the words "what is given in experience." If it were so intended, there would be some point in objecting that we don't have a very clear idea of what "immediately perceived" or "given" or "experience" mean. But in fact the phrases "immediately perceived" and "given in experience" are merely to function here as part of an attempt to indicate the denotation, not the sense, of the term "sense datum." The only real question is whether the attempt succeeds. It is relatively unimportant whether the reader knows what, if anything, is *meant* by "sense datum" as long as he has some idea of what those who use the term are talking *about*. Very few philosophers, I believe, will be able to say candidly that they have no such idea.

SUMMARY

This completes my discussion of the External World problem. I conclude that it has not been solved, and I believe that it never will be solved. Nor has anyone managed to "dissolve" it, either, whether by showing that in stating it we violate this or that convention or plausible principle concerning the proper use of language, or simply by talking us out of it without any explicit mention of the conventions or principles involved in the therapy. Further, I see no reason to suppose that projects to that end will be any more successful in the future than they have been in the past. I base these beliefs not only on the undeniable fact that no generally acceptable solution or dissolution has yet been achieved, after centuries of effort by an imposing array of philosophical talent, but also on a certain increasingly observable "permanence" in the problem: every clever attempt to solve it seems only to reveal that it is even deeper and more fundamental than it previously appeared to be.

That the major historical figures in the philosophical tradition have not been able to undo the knot is evident from their disagreements, and since their own refutations of one another are more effectively stated than any I could contrive, I have felt justified in keeping my historical comments to a very sketchy minimum. I have devoted proportionally more space to recent attacks upon the problem, which come for the most part from the direction of philosophy of language. To the charge that no purpose is served by "positing" such things as perceptions or sense data, the appropriate reply seems to be that whether or not something exists does not usually depend upon whether there is some purpose in our "positing" it—to which may be added the fact that, in any case, one cannot escape the External World problem merely by denying the existence of these suspect entities. To the claim that the hypothesis that there is no external world is, when properly understood, meaningless because absolutely unverifiable and even unconfirmable, the answer has to be that the verifiability criterion of meaning has never been stated in a way that would lead to this conclusion without at the same time excluding large classes of other sentences that are constantly in use and whose meaningfulness is intuitively unobjectionable. To the complaint that the epistemologists who have introduced the term "sense data" and its various associates have not succeeded in making us aware of what they are talking about, the response is a simple denial.

In fact, to complain that a typical sense-datum epistemologist like G. E. Moore, with his endless explanations ("When I say X, I *don't* mean Y_1, and I *don't* mean $Y_2, \ldots,$ and I *don't* mean Y_n, but I *do* mean Z_1, and I *do* mean $Z_2, \ldots,$ and I *do* mean Z_m"), is careless about the use of language is nothing short of preposterous. Clearly, it is not a characteristic of the successful use of language that every special term employed shall previously have been defined or explicated with maximum precision. Rather, we add Moore-like metalinguistic explanations if, as, and when the subject matter and other circumstances require. The word "tree," for example, ordinarily serves us well enough without any precise definition, but, when the dendrologist sets about writing a guidebook, he finds it necessary to sharpen the concept enough to permit differentiation of trees from shrubs, and for further purposes he would sharpen it still further.

It is a bit ironic that just those philosophers who sometimes delight in chiding logicians for paying inadequate attention to the flexibility and mutability of "living" language seem themselves in many respects to have an excessively rigid concept of it. Often they tell us authoritatively that "You *can't* say this" and "You *can't* say that," when the this and the that are precisely what large numbers of native speakers *do* say, managing without any difficulty to communicate with one another thereby. Thus, "I can perceive only my own perceptions" may sound linguistically odd at first hearing, and one might be inclined to retort "No, you perceive books and chairs and trees and the sky, but you don't perceive *perceptions.*" But after the epistemologist gives all his explanations of the word "perception," the proposition appears as a truism. It's too late then for the Ordinary Language philosopher to tell us, "But you *can't say* 'I am perceiving a perception.'" We *can* say it; we *do* say it; and it seems obviously true.

EPILOGUE

We have noted that the External World problem is a special case of a more general question, first raised by Hume, as to how one can have knowledge of the existence and nature of anything other than one's own experience of the present moment. This general problem begets a host of additional special cases and analogues. There is the problem of the continued existence of physical objects (even supposing that there are such): How do I know that the table in this room will continue to exist when I am no longer perceiving it? And the problem of the existence of other minds: How do I know that other people are not merely complex robots, who look and act as though they had a stream of experience similar to mine but really don't? And the problem of the existence of unperceived portions of perceived objects: How do I know that the tomato on the shelf has a far side, an inside, etc.? And the problem about surfaces that are almost "seen" to extend under the objects that rest upon them. And the problem about the past existence of oneself: How do I know that I didn't spring into existence a moment ago, replete with all my memories and the rest of the "evidence" that makes me so sure I have existed for quite a while? To unphilosophic minds these puzzles will doubtless seem just as silly as that concerning the External World. But they all have proved similarly resistant to solution, despite determined efforts by "the best minds."

The Free Will problem, too, has its variants and relatives. One of the most important ingredients in it is the principle that if you are not responsible for the cause you are not responsible for the effect. The "dual" of this, that if you *are* responsible for the cause you *are* at least to some extent responsible for the effect, generates difficulties of its own. On the one hand, it seems obvious that we must be held responsible for at least the "foreseeable" consequences, or effects, of that part of our total activity for which we do have responsibility. (If I light the fuse, I am surely responsible for the resulting explosion unless, acting under duress or in some other excusing circumstances, I was not responsible for the fuse-lighting either.) But what does "foreseeable" mean here? In the case of a given action, does it refer to the consequences that the agent actually *did* foresee, or those that he *ought* to have foreseen, or those that he *could* have foreseen (if . . . what?), or those that a "normal" person *would* have foreseen? None of these possible answers works out satisfactorily.

This problem, I suppose, essentially involves our basic intuition that usually the moral quality of an action depends in large measure upon the intent of the agent. But the verb "intended" is a notorious generator of oblique contexts, for which there is no adequate logic. From

He intended X

we cannot even infer

If $X = Y$, he intended Y

or

If X logically implies Y, he intended Y,

let alone

If X caused Y, he intended Y.

So intentions do not carry over from causes to effects, and yet we feel that people must in some sense be responsible for the effects of what they (responsibly) do.

There are many noticeable practical manifestations of the underlying conceptual tangle here. For just one example, consider the shifting uses of the terms "segregation" and "discrimination" in contemporary American sociopolitical discussion. To segregate schoolchildren according to race, i.e., to use ethnic origin as a criterion for determining where a child shall go to school, is undoubtedly disapproved by a large part of the population. On the other hand, the general policy of locating schools in such a way that each child will attend a school near his or her home is undoubtedly approved. But because of various circumstances, some deplorable and others not, people with similar ethnic backgrounds tend to live in the vicinity of one another. Consequently, the so-called neighborhood schools are often as racially unbalanced as if race had been used as a criterion for admission.

This state of affairs is then dubbed "de facto segregation," by a misuse of the de facto–de jure distinction,[1] and we read of cities and school districts being found "*guilty* of practicing de facto segregation." Behind that way of talking is the feeling that, whatever the policymakers' intentions may have been, the ultimate effect of their decisions is the same as if race had been used as the criterion, i.e., it is a segregated school system, the creation of which suffices to make the agents culpable. On the other side there is uneasiness about the use of pejorative terms like "segregation" and "guilt" in situations involving no evil intent. It is seen that, if we generalize this use of the expression "de facto"—with its implication that, if one's action has the same effect as a crime, then one has committed a species of that crime—all forms of killing will become de facto murder, smoking or overeating may become de facto suicide, and we shall have a whole new set of de facto crimes of which the unwary, and even the wary, may find themselves guilty. Both points of view have their plausibility because, paradoxically, the principle that responsibility for the cause implies responsibility for the effect seems both true and false.

Not only have these kinds of problems eluded solution, but nobody has found a really satisfactory way for the philosopher to reconcile himself to the fact that they are probably insoluble. As we have seen, the various attempts to escape the intellectual tension by theorizing that the problems themselves just do not make sense have been utter failures, and the problems continue to bother thoughtful people as much as they ever did. For it turns out that every supposed rule of language that is violated in their formulation is also constantly violated in the most ordinary and successful types of discourse and thus can hardly qualify as a rule at all.

Another suggestion for relief is found in the famous passage at the end of Hume's examination of what he calls "scepticism with regard to the senses":

> This sceptical doubt, both with respect to reason and the senses, is a malady, which can never be radically cured, but must return upon us every moment, however we may chase it away, and sometimes may seem entirely free from it. 'Tis impossible upon any system to defend either our understanding or senses; and we but expose them farther when we endeavor to justify them in that manner. As the sceptical doubt arises naturally from a profound and intense reflection on those subjects, it always increases, the farther we carry our reflections, whether in opposition or conformity to it. Carelessness and inattention alone can afford us any remedy. For this reason I rely entirely upon them; and

> take it for granted, whatever may be the reader's opinion at this present moment, that an hour hence he will be persuaded there is both an external and internal world.[2]

But, as is in effect admitted in the first sentence of this quotation, carelessness and inattention will not really be a very successful remedy. For, despite all the cant one hears to the contrary, man *is* a rational animal—he wants and needs to figure things out, get things straight; and the arguments of the skeptics, far from producing the promised *ataraxia,* leave him with feelings of intellectual discomfort and uneasiness that will not go away.

Because of its relation to practical matters the Free Will problem is even harder to live with than the External World problem. It has been suggested by some that, in the everyday business of apportioning praise and blame or rewards and punishment, we should cease trying to act in accord with general principles and should instead proceed on a "case-by-case" basis. Back of this suggestion is the claim that there *is* nothing common to all cases of action for which the agent is responsible; there are only so-called family resemblances, which we may utilize in classifying particular instances. That is, if *A*'s doing *X* is very much like *B*'s doing *Y* and the latter is a responsible action, then one is to classify the former action as responsible, too. But, we are told, don't look for a general rule with reference to which every case can be decided.

From this point of view, the mistake we have made in setting up the Free Will paradox (e.g., in its "excuses" form) is as follows. We have looked at a number of kinds of cases in which actions are excusable, and from these we have extracted or elicited a general principle, namely, that any action is excusable to the extent to which the causes of the action are not within the agent's power. Then, on the basis of some very natural and weak assumptions about causation, we have inferred that *every* action is excusable. The mistake lies in the general principle, for there is no general feature characterizing excusable actions; there is only a family resemblance.

This line of thought is really another proposal for solving or dissolving the paradox rather than a suggestion of how to live with it. In any case, it won't work. General applicability seems analytically involved in all moral concepts, including those of praise- and blameworthiness. That an individual *A* is worthy of blame for doing an act *X* if and only if anybody in the same circumstances would be equally blameworthy for doing *X* seems true by virtue of meanings alone. Further, if one is told "You shouldn't have done *X*," it is always in order to ask "Why not?"; and the reply "Because Smith, whose case is quite like yours, shouldn't have done *X*" will never be sufficient. One is always entitled to have one's case brought under some general rule. To show that one's action is wrong *is* to bring it under a principle or rule *P* such that every other case subsumable under *P* is also wrong, and the same holds for the concepts Right, Excusable, Praiseworthy, Blameworthy, etc. Hence there is really no such thing as "settling moral issues on a case-by-case basis." In short, while it is perhaps clear that the members of a family can bear a family resemblance to one another without there being any single feature that they all (or by large groups) have in common, morally qualified actions must be classified on principle.

In recent times the most frequently espoused way of coping with the Free Will paradox is to accept it as proving the bankruptcy of such concepts as freedom and responsibility and to propose a theory of reward and punishment that rests on an entirely different basis. According to this, in deciding whether to punish someone for an action, we are no longer to ask such questions as whether he is guilty or innocent, whether he acted freely or under some sort of constraint, and the like. Instead, we are to consider the overall social effects of the various alternatives before us. If incarcerating Smith for doing the harmful deed *X* will tend to deter others from similar behavior or will prevent Smith himself from committing crimes in the future, then we are to jail him without regard to the meaningless question of his guilt or innocence. Conversely, if there is no reason to believe that punishing him will bring about this or any other socially desirable consequences, then we are to let him off, again without regard to so-called guilt or innocence. Similarly, we are to reward Smith with a medal for a certain kind of desired behavior on the battlefield, even if we are convinced that he could hardly have done otherwise; we are in hopes that his fellow soldiers may thus be encouraged or actuated to behave in the same way.

This proposal, for all its apparent humaneness (we are no longer to think of so-called criminals as guilty, wicked, etc., but only as unfortunate victims of circumstance), flies too much in the face of our deepest moral intuitions. It is easy to imagine a case in which Smith, who in fact has not committed the terrible crime with which he is charged, is nevertheless universally believed to have done it; and we can add the supposition that a horde of potential criminals are watching anxiously to see whether he "gets away with it." Even if we assume in addition that failure to punish Smith will encourage these watchers to go out and commit the same crime themselves, while executing him will frighten them onto the path of virtue, it would be clearly and obviously unjust to treat an innocent man in this way. (I hardly need to add, I trust, that our offended intuitions in this matter cannot be mollified merely by redefining words in such a way that "*A* is innocent" comes simply to *mean* "no social purpose would be served by punishing *A*.")

The upshot is that here, too, Hume was probably right: there is no better prescription for coping with the problem than "carelessness and inattention." But this time the recommendation of inattention is even less practicable, for the issue is constantly put before us by difficulties we encounter in daily life. In the External World case one can perhaps console oneself with the fact that the problem, properly understood, has no practical implications whatever. But unfortunately the Free Will problem lacks even this saving feature. It seems that in practice we are forced to fall back on a kind of carelessness supplemented by ignorance, sometimes being ready to assign praise or blame, sometimes not, depending upon how well we happen to understand the causal sequences leading to the particular action in question. But such a modus vivendi, however necessary it may be to the man of action, can never be satisfactory to the philosopher.

Ridicula haec quaesitu sunt, sed difficilia explicatu. Plebs nos insanos putaret, si talia quaerentes audiret, et quaerenda sunt tamen.
Leibniz[3]

NOTES

Introduction

1. W. V. Quine, *The Ways of Paradox,* rev. ed. (Cambridge, Mass.: Harvard University Press, 1976), p. 7.
2. Ibid., p. 9.
3. Aristotle, *Physics* 263a.

Chapter One

1. Diogenes Laertius 2. 108. The standard work on the history of the Liar is Alexander Rüstow's *Der Lügner* (Leipzig: Teubner, 1910).
2. Athenaeus 9. 410E, as translated by St. George Stock in *Stoicism* (London: Constable, 1908), p. 36. See also Rüstow, *Der Lügner,* p. 101, where confirming testimony of Suidas is quoted.
3. Diogenes Laertius 5. 49. It should be mentioned that Aristotle himself hints at the Liar at *De Soph. El.* 180a32 ff., where he asks, "Is it possible for the same man at the same time to be a keeper and a breaker of his oath?" and then considers the man who swears that he will break his oath, adding that "the argument is similar, also, as regards the problem whether the same man can at the same time say what is both false and true."
4. Diogenes Laertius 7. 196–97.
5. Cicero, *Academica* 2. 95–96. Cf. Rüstow, *Der Lügner,* p. 40.
6. Alexander of Aphrodisias, *In Arist. Soph. El. Comm.,* ed. M. Wallies (Berlin, 1898), p. 171. Cf. Rüstow, *Der Lügner, p.* 41, where this version is ascribed to Michael of Ephesus.

7. See William Kneale and Martha Kneale, *The Development of Logic* (Oxford: Clarendon Press, 1962), pp. 227 ff.

8. See, e.g., the bibliography in Robert L. Martin, *The Paradox of the Liar* (New Haven: Yale University Press, 1970).

9. Epistle to Titus, 1:12–13, as translated in the New English Bible.

10. Diogenes Laertius, 1. 111.

11. Despite the nasty things Epimenides is supposed to have said about them, the Cretans in ancient times appear to have honored him as a god, and even now an important street in their principal city, Herakleion, bears his name.

12. See, for example, Peter Strawson, *Introduction to Logical Theory* (London: Methuen, 1952), pp. 3–4.

13. G. Ryle, "Heterologicality," *Analysis* 11 (1951): 67–68: "The same inattention to grammar is the source of such paradoxes as the Liar... When we ordinarily say 'That statement is false,' what we say promises a namely-rider, e.g., '... namely that today is Tuesday.' When we say 'The current statement is false,' we are pretending *either* that no namely-rider is to be asked for, *or* that the namely-rider is '... namely that the present statement is false.' If no namely-rider is to be asked for, then 'The current statement' does not refer to any statement... If, alternatively, it is pretended that there is indeed the namely-rider '... namely that the current statement is false,' the promise is met by an echo of that promise. If unpacked, our pretended assertion would run 'The current statement (namely that the current statement (namely that the current statement (namely that the current statement...' The brackets are never closed; no verb is ever reached; no statement of which we can ever ask whether it is true or false is ever adduced." Ryle's point seems to be based on a use-mention confusion, but in any case we can bypass it by replacing the demonstrative expression by a descriptive phrase for which no "namely-rider" is in any sense required.

14. A. Tarski, "The Semantic Conception of Truth," *Philosophy and Phenomenological Research* 4 (1944), sec. 7 and note 10. In order to avoid an ambiguous use of quotation marks, I have changed the formulation slightly.

15. Ibid., sec. 8 and note 11.

16. L. Wittgenstein, *Tractatus Logico-Philosophicus,* trans. D. F. Pears and B. F. McGuinness (London: Routledge & Kegan Paul, 1961): "3.332: No proposition can make a statement about itself, because a propositional sign cannot be contained in itself (that is the whole of the 'theory of types')."

17. Ibid., "3.121: Propositions cannot represent logical form: it

is mirrored in them. What finds its reflection in language, language cannot represent. What expresses *itself* in language, *we* cannot express by means of language. Propositions *show* the logical form of reality. They display it."

18. F. P. Ramsey, "Facts and Propositions," reprinted in *The Foundations of Mathematics* (Paterson, N.J.: Littlefield, Adams), p. 142: "it is evident that 'It is true that Caesar was murdered' means no more than that Caesar was murdered, and 'It is false that Caesar was murdered' means that Caesar was not murdered. They are phrases which we sometimes use for emphasis or for stylistic reasons, or to indicate the position occupied by the statement in our argument." A similar point was made by P. F. Strawson and others, who held that "true" has a primarily performative use, that of confirming or endorsing a statement.

19. This, of course, is essentially the method used by Tarski in "The Concept of Truth in Formalized Languages" (in A. Tarski, *Logic, Semantics, Metamathematics* [Oxford: Clarendon Press, 1956], pp. 152–278).

20. *Metaphysics* 1011b26 ff., trans. W. D. Ross.

21. S. Kripke, "Outline of a Theory of Truth," *Journal of Philosophy* 72 (1975): 695–96.

22. Strawson, *Introduction to Logical Theory*, pp. 174 ff.

23. For an exposition of this notion see, e.g., Gilbert Ryle, "Categories," in *Logic and Language*, 2d ser., ed. A. G. N. Flew (Oxford: Blackwell, 1959), pp. 65–81.

24. Kripke, "Outline of a Theory of Truth."

25. Ibid., p. 702.

26. See ibid., p. 700, note 18.

27. Similarly, a proposal by Bas van Fraassen ("Truth and Paradoxical Consequences," in *The Paradox of the Liar*, ed. R. L. Martin [New Haven: Yale University Press, 1970], pp. 13–23) leads, if I have understood it correctly, to the result that neither *A* nor the sentence

A is true

nor

A is not true

is true, though *A* is neither true nor false.

28. Brian Skyrms, "Return of the Liar," *American Philosophical Quarterly* 7 (1970): 153–61. See also the same author's "Notes on Quantification and Self-Reference," in R. L. Martin, ed., *The Paradox of the Liar*, pp. 67–74.

29. William Kneale, "Russell's Paradox and Some Others,"

British Journal for the Philosophy of Science 23 (1971): 321.

30. G. Frege, "On Sense and Reference," in *Translations from the Philosophical Writings of Gottlob Frege,* trans. P. Geach and M. Black (Oxford: Basil Blackwell, 1952), p. 59.

31. I may be unfair to Russell here. In *An Inquiry into Meaning and Truth* (London: Allen & Unwin, 1940), he defines (p. 176) "proposition" as "the significance of a sentence," and (pp. 189 ff.) he gives a psychological analysis of significance. He also says (p. 188) that what he means by "proposition" is the "implicit behavior" of the hearer when a corresponding sentence (in his language) is uttered.

32. My doubts about the concept of Statement are set forth at length in "Austin, Strawson, Tarski, and Truth," in *Proceedings of the Tarski Symposium* (Providence, R.I.: American Mathematical Society, 1974), pp. 385–96.

33. In a certain village there is a barber who has a monopoly on shaving, i.e., he shaves all those and only those inhabitants of the village who do not shave themselves. Therefore, he shaves himself if and only if he does not shave himself.

34. Note that in this section I am letting the letter "*S*" *name* a sentence; in formulation (3) of the Liar, I let the letter "*A*" *abbreviate* a descriptive phrase that named a sentence.

35. A. Fraenkel, article "Set Theory," *Encyclopedia of Philosophy*, 8 vols. (New York: Macmillan, 1967). For references to other definitions given by Cantor see Fraenkel's *Einleitung in die Mengenlehre* (Berlin: Springer), p. 4, n. 1.

36. E.g., P. R. Halmos, *Naive Set Theory* (Princeton: Van Nostrand, 1960), p. 1: "A pack of wolves, a bunch of grapes, or a flock of pigeons are all examples of sets of things."

37. For an introduction to the enormous literature on this subject, see the bibliography in A. A. Fraenkel and Y. Bar-Hillel, *Foundations of Set Theory* (Amsterdam: North-Holland, 1959).

38. Similarly, one of the linguistic rules prohibits the use of quantifiers that are unrestricted as to type, while the ontological account runs "Everything there is, is either an individual, or a class of individuals, or a class of classes of individuals, or. . . ."

39. It is of course possible to describe the division of names and variables into types without making any reference to the individuals or other entities they are supposed to denote or range over.

40. See note 23, above.

41. Thus Kurt Gödel, writing in *The Philosophy of Bertrand Russell,* ed. P. A. Schilpp (New York: Tudor, 1944), p. 131, says: "By analyzing the paradoxes to which Cantor's set theory had led, he

to exist when we shut our eyes. But it would be a mistake to infer that they are dependent upon mind, not real while we see them, or not the sole basis for our knowledge of the external world."

5. All of this follows from the Humean principle that whatever impressions, ideas, or objects are *distinguishable* are also *separable*.

6. See M. Schlick, "Meaning and Verification," in *Readings in Philosophical Analysis*, ed. H. Feigl and W. Sellars (New York: Appleton-Century-Crofts, 1949), p. 163.

7. With some justification it might be replied to this that *saying* such a thing might be *odd* but that what was said would not necessarily be *false*. Indeed, it could be argued that in the typical situation in which the evidence *T* makes *S* highly probable but does not logically imply it the odd assertion would actually be true. The response to this is Berkeley's observation next cited in the text.

8. See Austin's "Other Minds," *Philosophical Papers*, p. 83. This use of italics seems to give particular satisfaction to the ordinary-language or common-sense type of dogmatist but to have no beneficial effect whatever on skeptics.

9. W. V. Quine, *The Ways of Paradox* (Cambridge, Mass.: Harvard University Press, 1976), p. 229.

10. In the following historical section I have for the most part omitted to cite texts, assuming that the views I am ascribing to the various authors are well-enough known. I recognize the danger in this, but I am reluctant to bring in the whole apparatus that would be required for a more scholarly treatment.

11. Berkeley, *Works*, vol. 1, pp. 260–61.

12. G. Santayana, *Scepticism and Animal Faith* (New York: Charles Scribner's Sons, 1923), p. 106.

13. J. L. Austin, *Sense and Sensibilia* (Oxford: Clarendon Press, 1962), p. 17: "we should *not* say we see the guns indirectly, if we see in the distance only the flashes of guns." But consider the following dialogue:

> (To spotter) Do you see the guns?
> No. No. Wait a minute! Yes! I *do* see them!
> Are they 88s?
> Well, actually I see only the flashes, so I can't tell.

Now would there be anything particularly odd about saying, of that situation, that "In a sense he sees the guns, though *strictly speaking* he sees only the flashes" or even "He sees only the flashes directly, and he supposes that these flashes are the flashes of guns"?

14. The reason why it is difficult to refute people who say that sense data are brain-states is the same as the reason why it would be difficult to refute someone who maintained, e.g., that hummingbirds are positive integers. To show that *A* is different from *B*, one tries to find a predicate that is true of *A* but false of *B*; but this involves finding a predicate that can *meaningfully* be applied to both.

15. Of course one might try to pin the responsibility on "same" or "thing," but it is dangerous to tamper with expressions that are located so near to the logical heart of our discourse.

16. Or for a person to see what he hears.

17. W. V. Quine, *Word and Object* (Cambridge, Mass.: M.I.T. Press, 1960), pp. 234 ff.

18. Ryle, *The Concept of Mind,* pp. 217 ff.

19. J. L. Austin, *Sense and Sensibilia* (Oxford: Clarendon Press, 1962).

20. M. Schlick, "The Foundation of Knowledge," trans. D. Rynin, in *Logical Positivism,* ed. A. J. Ayer (Glencoe, Ill.: Free Press, 1959), p. 225.

21. C. Hempel, "The Empiricist Criterion of Meaning," in *Logical Positivism* (see preceding note), p. 110.

22. Ibid., p. 111. Hempel has "finite consistent set" instead of "consistent set," but in view of compactness the qualification "finite" is superfluous.

23. A. J. Ayer, *Language, Truth and Logic* (London: Gollancz, 1936; 2d ed. 1946).

24. Alonzo Church, *Journal of Symbolic Logic* 14 (1949): 52–53.

25. See, e.g., Hempel, "The Empiricist Criterion of Meaning," pp. 117 ff.

26. G. A. Paul, "Is There a Problem about Sense Data?" *Proceedings of the Aristotelian Society,* suppl. vol. 15 (1936): 61–77.

27. Ibid., pp, 61–62.

28. Ibid., p. 65.

29. Ryle, *The Concept of Mind,* p. 217.

30. J. L. Austin, "Are There A Priori Concepts?" in *Philosophical Papers,* p. 17; also, *Sense and Sensibilia,* pp. 15 ff., 87 ff., 136.

31. G. Frege, "On Sense and Reference," in *Translations from the Philosophical Writings of Gottlob Frege,* trans. P. Geach and M. Black (Oxford: Basil Blackwell, 1952).

32. Ibid., p. 58.

EPILOGUE

1. I here rely on etymology rather than on what the law may

say. We are talking *about* the law, not *in* the law. To say that an action is such-and-such de jure is to say that it is classified as such-and-such by the law; to say that it is such-and-such de facto is to say that it *is* such-and-such (whether or not it is so classified by the law). The distinction is not one between *intended* and *intended-or-not* but between *according to law* and *in fact, whether according to law or not.*

2. D. Hume, *A Treatise of Human Nature,* ed. L. A. Selby-Bigge (Oxford: Clarendon Press, 1888), p. 218.

3. The quotation is from the Academy edition of Leibniz's *Works,* II. i. 63.

INDEX